Life in the Stress Lane

HOW TO TOLERATE PEOPLE & PROBLEMS

2nd Edition

DR. STUART ATKINS

SURVIVE ♦ ACHIEVE ♦ PROSPER

Published by Ashford Publishing

Notice:
This book is designed to provide information and as a reference in regard to the subject matter covered. It is sold with the understanding that it is informational and educational and is not intended as a substitute for medical, psychological, or career services. If your problems require professional services, a competent professional should be sought.

Ashford Publishing
8306 Wilshire Blvd. #990
Beverly Hills, CA 90211
1-323-650-5097
www.stresslane.com

International Standard Book Number
ISBN: 978-0-9796275-0-7
Library of Congress Cataloging-in-Publication Data

CONTENTS

Preface—Exhaust in the Stress Lane **6**
Acknowledgements **7**
Introduction **9**
Living with Uncertainty and Change

Part I
Life in the Stress Lane

Chapter 1

The Stress Lane **13**
Racing from People and Problems
Three Markers in the Stress Lane 15
First Marker in the Stress Lane—
Encountering Trouble 15
Second Marker—Numbed by Trouble 16
Third Stress Marker—Drained by
the Trouble 17
Connecting Stress to Everyday Problems 18
Measuring Our Troubling Problems.......................18
Old Stress Management—Medicate, Meditate,
Exercise, and Relax 19

Chapter 2

Obstacles in the Stress Lane..................................... **21**
People and Problems
Typical Stressful Events 22
Stressful People 23
Stressful Characteristics 23

Stressful Organizations 24
Self-Generated Problems and Stress......................25
Old Reactions in New Events 28
Triggers to Old Reactions 28
New Double Lane Stress Model 29

Chapter 3

Distress Signals When We Are Frustrated or Unhappy 32

Recognizing the Signals in What We Do

Beyond Fight-Flight When We "See" Danger 34
Behavior That Signals We Are Stressed and Unhappy 34
Case History: The Unhappy Supervisor 39

Part II
How to Tolerate People

Chapter 4

Taking Stressful People in Stride 43

Why People Rub Us the Wrong Way

Stressful Characteristics 44
Why Stressful Characteristics Rub Us the Wrong Way 46
Positive Source of Negative Behavior.............. 55
Stuck on the Negative 56
Searching for the Middle Ground 56
3 Stages of Behavior 57

Chapter 5

The Four Temptations 60

Self-Generated Problems and Stress

'Supporting' Temptations 61

'Controlling' Temptations 62

'Conserving' Temptations 63

'Adapting' Temptations 64

Breaking Free From Temptations 65

Pleasure But Not Too Much—Just Right 65

The 1, 2, 3 of Self-Generated Stress 66

Affirm and Guide Technique 67

Part III
How to Tolerate Problems

Chapter 6

Tolerating Perplexing Problems 75

Tolerance Techniques in Action

Consolation—Misery Loves Company 78

Outer Limits—It's Not Forever.............................81

Silver Lining—The Good News in the Bad 83

Reward Yourself—A Carrot on a Stick..................85

Nothing Personal—Take the "I" Out...................86

Comic Relief—Timeout from Trouble 92

Which Tolerance Techniques Will Work Best for You? 96

Try Out Section 98

Chapter 7

Give Problems the Third Degree 106

Probing Questions That Produce Solutions

Solutions Techniques 106

Testing Probabilities 108

Replace Ill-logics 111

Reducing Old Reactions 118

Find Overlooked Alternatives 121

Try Out Section 127

Chapter 8

Past Problems in the Present....................................139

The Shadow and the Fly

Old Reactions in New Events 140

Triggers to Old Reactions 140

The Case of the Boss Who Couldn't Be Pleased 140

The Case of Coworkers with an Attitude 143

The Case of the Fence-Sitting In-Laws 145

Part IV
How to Tolerate Relationships

Chapter 9

Stress and The Myth of Compatibility 151

Four Patterns of Living and Loving

The Myth of Compatibility.................................. 152

Couples, Kaleidoscopes, and Compatibility... 152

Basic Patterns of Living and Loving.................. 153

Little and Big Problems That Create Stress........ 159

Typical Problems—Little Ones 159
Typical Problems—Big Ones 160
Which is Better—Having the Same or Different Patterns? 161
Four Patterns of Fighting and Making Up 162

Chapter 10
Couple Patterns and Relationship Stress 167
Attractions, Problems, and Solutions
Being Alike—Problems and the Work To Be Done 167
Being Different—Attractions, Problems, and the Work To Be Done 178
Simple Complexity 193

Suggested Readings 194
About the Author 195
Workshop Information 197
Ordering Information 198

PREFACE

EXHAUST IN THE STRESS LANE

When people and problems confront us, our body mobilizes its energy. We're on alert, focused for action! If the people and problems are not better tolerated, or the problems not solved, often our body stays on alert prepared for the worst.

The energy from this alert state has no place to go outside of the body and can be very wearing. It is like the accelerator of a parked car being stuck, continuously running the car's engine but without its exhaust system and tail pipe.

Attempts to relieve our trapped "exhaust" are recreation, vacations, and stress reduction techniques like medication, relaxation, visualization and exercise.

But what generates the exhaust in the first place? Problems do. Problems from events and people fuel the stress and must be solved or successfully tolerated. If we only drain off our exhaust with stress reduction techniques, we will be overlooking the primary problems that regenerate and recycle the stress.

When we learn to tolerate or solve the problems causing the stress, we in effect lift the accelerator, slow down the engine, and reduce the amount of exhaust. This also reduces the wear and tear on our body and brain. Life in the stress lane can be less tiring and more satisfying when we better tolerate people and problems.

Dr. Stuart Atkins, 2009
Beverly Hills, California

ACKNOWLEDGEMENTS

As my consulting firm flourished in the US, and my activity expanded, I began to realize how much stress played a part in relationships, careers and organizational life. The pioneering work of Dr. Hans Selye, particularly his book "Stress Without Distress," stimulated some important insight into my own stress. It also sparked my interest in developing a new stress program.

A client, Dr. Tony Torres, an organizational trainer and physician in a hospital group, helped me develop an early version of my stress course with emphasis on the physical consequences of stress and how to reduce its physical symptoms.

In time, my stress course evolved to problem solving techniques, solving the problems causing the stress in the first place, before the onset of physical symptoms. The stress program is called Solve It!—Solving Stressful Problems.

Thanks go to Dr. Diane Sukiennik and Dr. Scott Wimer who helped develop training materials for my early stress workshops, and to Diane for her friendship, excellent counsel, and pioneering effort as a teacher in the initial stress workshops.

Also thanks to David Glowatzke, a master trainer for my former consulting company, who became the master trainer for the stress program and provided helpful feedback about what was most useful to participants and how to improve the program.

Eric Dahl, for twenty years, was my Vice President of Program Development, and to him I acknowledge my appreciation for his friendship, intelligence, and know-how in program development and instructional methods.

As my customer services manager, Marcia Johnson has been an enthusiastic supporter of the stress program to client companies and in her own family. Her insight and sense of the market place—what people need and want—has been valuable and on the mark.

To Mr. Shogo Saito, Chairman of Business Consultants, Inc., one of the largest consulting and training companies in Japan, there are thanks for his vision and leadership for global expansion for the company's programs and services and incorporating my work in that expansion.

Thanks to Valerie Delker, my editor, who provided me with encouragement and wise counsel on the tone, style, and organization of this book.

I also appreciate the work of Doreen Barnes for the page by page look of the book and for her patience in incorporating my on-going changes.

On the personal side, I thank my wife Allison who patiently endured my absence while I was at the computer, yet continually reminded me that a book is not a book until it is in the hands of readers.

Dr. Stuart Atkins, 2009
Beverly Hills, California

INTRODUCTION

Living with Uncertainty and Change

In today's unpredictable world, our stress or vulnerability to stress is heightened by events that confront us with ever increasing frequency and impact. Though these represent a wide variety of stressful events, many of them have one thing in common—CHANGE.

Something new and different will be required of us. This means uncertainty, which is not a state we relish. In fact, the unknown represents one of the most universal fears. There may be danger in uncertainty—real or imagined—and we are more likely to see, think and expect the worst. There can be no more fertile field for creating stress than uncertainty.

Notwithstanding today's reality, there are still many events within our own control. For those out of our control, we can learn to better tolerate them and increase our productivity and satisfaction, in spite of them.

That's what this book is all about, control—how to control our own tolerance level for people, problems, and change in our stressful world.

There are daily factors that contribute to our feeling of being out of control. While technology and easy credit had transformed our homes into a showplace of entertainment, convenience, and communication, now, for many of us, that is disappearing and has left us in a state of uncertainty.

Remember back in the 1980s, to simplify our lives, came the computer. Less paper was the promise, along with saving time to do other things. Yes, other things on the computer. Software manufactures figured out clever applications and programs to keep us busy and entertained. We were uncertain but hopeful.

At least the time spent with the computer reduced our TV viewing time from the couch. But we can now hook TV right to our computer. That's progress—we're off the couch! Or at least we were until the wireless network, and now we are back on the couch freed from the desktop by our wireless laptop linked to our home network.

Let us not forget our wonderful internet service providers and the many software technicians with whom we have frequent "enlightening" conversations. It is like a travelogue, we talk to out-sourced technicians in Canada, Florida, India, Scotland, and Seattle. Frequently, we get promoted from the first level technician to a more advanced one, who finally tells us to call the hardware manufacturer, who tells us to talk to the software company. "Deal with it!" is the implied message.

Uncertainty extended to trips to the doctor's office. The visit could make you sick. Medical practice with the drug solutions can cure us if the side effects don't kill us. We are gamblers—oh, the thrill of uncertainty.

When we see the doctor, we have a five minute audience to tell our woes, be "examined," be diagnosed, and written up on that tiny prescription pad to make all the uncertainty go away.

With a little luck, our problems can be corrected. If not, we are referred to a specialist who completely contradicts the first doctor's diagnosis, prescribes different pills and promises to call our primary physician. We never hear anything about it again.

On the personal side, compounding uncertainty, there are love affairs to fall in and out of, divorces, death in the family, voluntary or involuntary change of jobs, parents and children to care for, relationships to mend or find, and decisions about what to buy and buy.

To help us with our uncertainty and its problems, gone are many of our familiar heroes who, in our fantasies, would keep us from danger and take care of all our problems. Many have been struck down by their own misfortune and miscalculation. Many are infamous now.

Though they excelled at sports or politics or the arts or business, they are fallen idols, pushed off their pedestals by the pressures and stress of modern life—and the swift revelations of modern media.

Our presidents, up until now, have been diminished, stripped of their omnipotence to take care of us by the political process. Each new president holds out the promise to save us from harm as we cynically wait for the next disillusioning revelation.

Our new president Obama reminds us that we can no longer completely rely on the borrowed strength and power of heroes, nor of the government. Besides government policies and programs, we are on our own, and life is now a do-it-yourself kit. It always has been but now it is more difficult to deny.

If we want to be rescued, we can't look to Superman, Wonder Woman, or the government alone. They have their own troubles. We have to depend on ourselves. We have to be our own super men and wonder women and have our own recovery plan and deal with the uncertainty.

How do we face our uncertainty, changes, our stressful people and problems, and the demands of contemporary life in the stress lane? For one thing, we need a "pit stop" to check ourselves out. We need to take time to think and reflect about how we are doing. And we need to determine what repairs and service we need to keep us going, to win the race. It can be done.

Let me share with you what I discovered about how to survive, achieve, and prosper in the stress lane.

Stuart Atkins, Ph. D.
Beverly Hills, California, 2009

Part I

Life in the Stress Lane

CHAPTER 1

THE STRESS LANE

Racing from People and Problems

On a vacation, I was driving my car down a deserted highway. I turned off the air conditioning and lowered the windows to take advantage of the day. The sky was clear and blue, the air fresh and cool. Routinely, I looked into the rearview mirror. This time, I noticed a car behind me. I had an eerie sense that the car was following me. I stepped on the accelerator and pulled away. But the car caught up.

As I tightened my grip on the steering wheel, a surge of energy alerted my body. I stepped harder on the accelerator. The car behind increased its speed. There were two men in the car. One reached into the back seat and grabbed a long object. "It's a shotgun!" I said to myself.

Every muscle in my shoulders tightened. I could feel my heart beating faster. My eyes were fixed straight ahead on the highway. I pushed the accelerator to the floor.

Up ahead, on the side of the highway, two people were waving their hands. For an instant, I thought about stopping and getting their help. But before I could react, I was past them.

As I swerved around a curve, I saw a sign with large red letters: "Bridge Out! Danger."

Approaching the bridge, I slowed down. The car behind me pulled up alongside. Looking straight ahead, but from the corner of my eye, I saw the front window of the other car moving down. I decided to face them eye to eye. Slowly, I turned my head toward them.

A gruff, unshaven man looked me in the eyes and asked, "Can you tell us the direction to the lake? We're lost."

I turned and leaned my body toward them and shouted out the window, "You're what!?"

The man was startled. He responded with hesitation. "Ah, I said, 'lost.' I think we're lost. We've been trying to catch up with you to find out where the lake is."

Angered from fright, I shot back, "Where it's always been!"

I quickly scanned the inside of the other car. I saw fishing poles and tackle boxes. What I thought was a shotgun turned out to be a collapsed fishing pole in a canvas cover.

"You'll have to forgive me," I apologized. "I got a little upset while you were trying to catch up. Maybe those people back around the bend would know where the lake is. I guess they were trying to flag us down … warn us about the bridge."

The lost fishermen turned around and headed back toward the people on the highway.

I slumped in the driver's seat. All my flight-fight protective energy spent, I felt like I had been through a close race. I sighed and took a breath. I started laughing in relief.

Three Markers in the Stress Lane

How stress accelerates in stressful events, as mine did with the fishermen, was identified by the pioneer of stress research, Hans Selye, and described in his book, *The Stress of Life,* 1957. He called our stress reactions the General Adaptation Syndrome (G.A.S.). The G.A.S. is simply a series of three stages we all experience after we are stressed by **perceived** physical or psychological danger.

First Marker in the Stress Lane—Encountering Trouble

Hans Selye called the first marker of trouble: **Alarm**.

Any situation, or action by another person, which is perceived by us as threatening to our physical or psychological well-being, triggers the alarm. Our primitive brain, the hypothalamus, signals our body to get ready to act, and we respond with all sorts of physical reactions. For example, our hearts beat quicker, hormones in our blood send sugar to the muscles and brain for extra energy, and our breathing quickens to take in more oxygen. We can sweat or go cold. We become "hot under the collar" or develop "cold feet."

Depending upon the nature and seriousness of the threat, we can rise to the occasion quickly. When we handle the event, cope with the emergency, or solve the problem, the threat is gone. Our body returns to a state of equilibrium and the physical side effects of the stress state subside. We've coped.

Second Marker—Numbed by Trouble

But if we don't cope with the problem, the threat continues. In this case, we can enter the second stage of stress: **Saturation.**

In this stage, our body reactions continue at a high level to keep us in a defensive stress state. Our muscles can stay tense, heart rate stays quickened, blood pressure remains high, and the hormones in our blood keep sending sugar to our muscles and brain for extra energy.

We take our exaggerated effort for granted. We have "forgotten" how we felt before the problem. But we are borrowing from the future. We are so busy dealing with the stressful event or stressful person that we no longer notice our bodily reactions. It feels like second nature. Haven't we always been this way? We have become numbed by our intensity.

Third Stress Marker—Drained by the Trouble

If the stress continues unattended, our sharpened edge of awareness may blunt, and we begin to feel inadequate to the task. We feel frustrated and angry, perhaps depressed. What follows is the feeling of distress. Unrelieved stress piled on stress can lead to distress, says Hans Selye, the father of stress research. Stress stimulates, but too much stress debilitates. No matter how briefly, we've temporarily "burned out."

We are now in the third stage of stress: **Exhaustion.**

We are like the light bulb that has a surge of light and then burns out, leaving a smoky gray film where light used to be. Now we finally realize what has happened to us. Something is not right. We feel so weary.

What is stressful for me may not be stressful for you. Our alarms may be different, or the same alarm may have to clang louder for one of us to hear it. For some of us, only a faint sound of a particular alarm sets us off.

Therefore, my definition of stress: An intense physiological state within the brain and body which occurs when we react with alarm to physical or psychological danger—real or imagined—from problems caused by events or people.

Another example of stress from physical danger would be if I were walking down the street and I saw a big man approaching me, talking loudly and irrationally. My body would respond with an alert state to prepare me to protect myself. Now I could either dash across the street (flight), or stay on my side of the street and take him on if he started trouble (fight).

Stress from psychological danger would be more subtle. Suppose a rumor has been circulating that the boss is against the idea you have proposed. In a meeting, as he begins to respond to your idea, your body tenses up to protect you from possible rejection and embarrassment. You could decide whether to argue your case and vigorously defend your position (fight), or shrug your shoulders and say to yourself that the idea wasn't important anyway (flight).

Connecting Stress to Everyday Problems

Like my vacation experience of being "pursued" by the fishermen, all of us are symbolically chased everyday down the stress lane. It's not by a car but by problems stemming from events and people. If it seems these problems are going to "catch up" with us or overtake us, our body mobilizes its forces. We're on alert to take action!

Then we jam the accelerator to the floor and race our engine, prepared to take flight. Or, we may pull over to the side and prepare to fight, or maybe just sit there and fret, or frustrate ourselves and others by analyzing and analyzing and analyzing what to do next.

Measuring Our Troubling Problems

US Naval Captain Richard Rahe, a medical doctor, first presented his research findings on stress more than 30 years ago. He had studied the physical and medical consequences of stress on navy personnel at their San Diego naval base. Included in his study were numerous medical tests monitoring physical and chemical changes in the body. One of the best indicators of stress, he found, was the level of uric acid in a subject's body. Sustained high levels of uric acid could foreshadow serious illness.

Rahe also inquired about his subjects' life circumstances. What was happening in their lives appeared to have a direct connection to the significant results of the medical tests. He sorted out these circumstances through the Recent Life Changes questionnaire, ranking recent changes in importance according to how important his subjects viewed their impact.

The life changes ranged in severity from the death of someone close, to a divorce, loss of a job, a change of social activities, to getting a traffic ticket. His conclusion was that the stress level from an accumulation of these events could cause serious medical consequences. Eventually, Rahe could predict which subjects in his study would eventually become ill.

At his presentation at UCLA in 1975, he distributed to us a "Recent Life Changes" questionnaire, which he co-authored. Those who scored 150 points or less were "low risk" to become ill, with 150 to 300 points "intermediate risk" was one's fate, but with more than 300 points one was classified as "high risk" to have medical problems.

And so began my involvement with the study of stress. My questionnaire score showed that I was in the "intermediate risk" category. I can't say that I was pleased or even relieved. I was diagnosed, but what was the treatment plan? What was I to do?

Old Stress Management—Medicate, Meditate, Exercise, and Relax

My stress gathered more momentum as I researched health-oriented articles and courses. They emphasized how a "fast track" job and a "Type A" personality destined me for a myocardial infarction, ulcers, chronic fatigue syndrome or at least a generally impaired immune system.

These scare tactics did not help me. If anything, they amplified my stress because I still didn't know what to do to reverse course. People I interviewed in organizations felt the same. They were wary about stress programs, particularly after participating in one! With all that emphasis on health problems, people were of one mind: "If you don't want to be stressed, don't take a stress course!"

My stress level took another hike after my annual physical examination that year. I discovered that my blood pressure was too high. That was a surprise and a disappointment since I was proud of being in top physical condition. I believed I had the body of a much younger man.

My doctor prescribed pills for my pressure. After experiencing some unpleasant side effects from the medication, I stopped the drug therapy. Relaxation techniques were becoming popular, so I tried hard to relax—a contradiction in terms. I was so active that I didn't have the patience for these more passive techniques.

Biofeedback was another promising tool that I tried. When I was hooked up to the tension measuring equipment, which beeped progressively more softly as I relaxed, I could reduce my stress state. But when I got back to the office, I faced the same problems and frustrations. Zap! In no time my relaxed state surrendered to the problems and stress.

CHAPTER 2

OBSTACLES IN THE STRESS LANE

People and Problems

As an applied behavioral scientist, I decided to bypass the physical and medical approaches to stress and focus on what causes stress in the first place—and how to eliminate it at its source! I wanted to know more about the impact of stress on people's relationships and performance, not just their health. I wanted to develop practical techniques to preserve—even improve—performance and relationships under stress.

My goal was to have us better tolerate people and problems to gain more confidence and mastery over roadblocks in the stress lane.

As I field-tested the early version of my new stress program, participants freely spoke about their stressful problems both at home and at work. They said these events push their panic buttons. Some of these I have listed below.

Typical Stressful Events

Which of these stressful events do you find most stressful?

- Searching for a job
- Insufficient funds to pay bills
- Transfer or promotion does not come through
- Project canceled in the middle
- A new boss arrives
- Major purchase and financial obligation
- Death or illness in the family
- Assume care of a parent
- Change in working hours
- Must learn to use new equipment
- Receive negative or unfair performance review
- Not enough time for yourself
- Conflicting demands at home and work
- Rumor that the company will be sold
- Forced to work more quickly and raise output
- Separation from a significant person
- Discipline or receive a formal warning
- Not included in an important social gathering
- Change in living conditions
- Promotion given to a peer based on politics
- Policy and procedures change
- Lose a prestigious responsibility
- Start a new job
- Denied time off or vacation time
- Illness or accident restricts activity

- Child gets into trouble
- Reorganization in progress
- Spend too much time in meetings
- Work group loses some major resources
- Conflict between your group and another
- Overqualified or underqualified for the job

It becomes evident that many of these problem events cannot be solved immediately. In those cases, tolerance is necessary. And further, since some problems cannot be solved at all, tolerance also is required on a continuous basis. Therefore, we need to learn to live better with problem events, and in a way that means less stress.

People in my workshops looked at the complete list of stressful events and realized that many events impacted them with varying degrees of stress. So I had people select only a few events that were most stressful. Surprisingly, after they found solutions to problems in one stressful event, their confidence spilled over to the other events on their list. Now they seemed less urgent and more tolerable.

But problems were untouched by medication, meditation, or relaxation. These old stress management approaches alleviated the immediate impact of stress on the body, but they did not solve the problems!

Stressful People

After dealing with stressful events, workshop participants wanted to deal with the impact of stressful people. So I drew upon twenty-five years of consulting experience in which I helped organizations resolve relationship problems. I also drew upon experiences from my Life Orientations® program to identify a list of characteristics that have a stressful impact on other people.[1]

The list generated high-energy discussions among participants in workshops, as if they had stored months or years of frustration about these characteristics and suddenly could release it. Reactions ranged from irritation to exasperation to anger. Some of the characteristics on the list were:

Stressful Characteristics

Self-effacing	Nit-picking
Gullible	Passive
Data-bound	Over-analytical
Domineering	Wishy-washy
Impatient	Approval-seeking
Arrogant	Inconsistent
Impulsive	Placating
Overprotective	Plodding

Not all characteristics were equally stressful for everyone. The characteristics that stressed some people were easily dismissed by others. Which of those characteristics stress you? Can you add some to the list?

For me, it was people who became wishy-washy and inconsistent. Because of my own way of working, I preferred people to be direct with me, no backpedalling. And if they said something today and switched their story tomorrow, they lost credibility with me. When I was forced to work with them on some important project, I was impatient and stressed.

---

[1] Life Orientations, The Lifo Method, for short, is available in the USA from The Schutz Company, New York and Agents worldwide. www.poweredbylifo.com.

Stressful Organizations

A giant, successful company in the software business and related fields is an example of the new speed of change. Stress is a built in by-product in the company's constant state of flux. It is keeping up with innovation and leading innovation at the same time. As a result, reorganizations create a continual shift of assignments and bosses. It is possible that one could change office space four or five times a year and change bosses every one or two years. Top management seems to treat the organization as a product, something to tinker with and improve, like a new software version 5.3.1.

July and August are the change months following the fiscal year end in June. During the changes, employees share their assessments of the bosses who are the good managers and the not so good and those to avoid at all cost. Aware and skillful employees network and seek out the "good guys" to lobby for assignments on their team. When the manager is reassigned, the employee will seek a transfer and follow that manager to his or her next assignment.

There is a mandatory time commitment of one year on assignments and if an employee happens to get a "bad" manager, the calendar is marked with X indicating time served and time to go—an old-fashioned stress reduction technique. One employee described his assignment with a manager as "beyond miserable" and had many physical and psychological symptoms from the stress. After he served his mandatory time and changed managers, all his symptoms disappeared!

This organization is far from heartless. People are devoted and feel they are on a crusade into the future. They do work on weekends and on vacations. And a stress clinic is available to all. Each year there is a survey of life/work balance, and each year the results are the same. There is an imbalance on the side of work. But the individual satisfactions from technical creativity, the organization's mission and status in the marketplace seems compensatory for the stress.

Self-Generated Problems and Stress

Looking outside of ourselves for the source of our stress is a natural and helpful perspective. But it is much more difficult to look within ourselves to find this little recognized but frequent source of stress.

Consider this. Our favorite patterns of living, working, and loving give us enduring pleasure. We feel like our true selves, doing what comes naturally. The temptation is to experience this pleasure wherever and whenever we can.

There are four temptations:

HELPING: Giving our all with high standards, trying to be a worthy and helpful person.

DOING: Taking what we need to get quick results and moving on to the next challenge.

THINKING: Holding on to what works and planning future effort a step at a time with facts and figures.

PLEASING: Dealing and compromising to keep things running smoothly and influencing with a light touch.

For example, the pleasure in our patterns may lead us to seek responsibility and work harder than others to meet our high standards, while helping others to do the same. Or, we can get quick results with a challenging project never done before, rallying and directing people to get behind it. Some of us get pleasure from laying out a plan with alternatives based on what worked well before, and with a timetable for each step of the way. Others may find pleasure in smoothing over tense situations with a light touch and finding ways for everyone to compromise, especially when all are pleased with the solution and us.

Those are some of our tempting pleasures. That's us. We love it! Therefore, why not do as much of it as possible? It's so confirming and pleasurable.

But there can be too much of a good thing. Our pleasure can be someone else's displeasure. Others can sense the self-serving nature of our efforts and feel put upon, and react negatively to stop us.

What's more, perhaps the task at hand does not require so much hard work, quick action, extensive analysis, or that much compromise. What comes naturally to us may not be what is naturally required in a particular situation. Nevertheless, we pour our time and energy into it, often letting other projects pile up. But because our favorite patterns give us such pleasure, we don't think twice about whether our actions can lead to overload and stress.

Pleasure wins out.

We have created stress by reducing the time we have for our many other pressing responsibilities. Underlying time management is managing the temptations.

Old Reactions in New Events

To complete my stress model I included some old reactions that we carry around with us to every event and every encounter with people. These old reactions are from earlier bad experiences, and they compound and inflame our stress.

Whenever we feel stressed from events or people, we can have one or several of these old reactions hovering in the background, wanting to get into the act. When they do, they intensify our stress and the original problem takes longer to solve. Even when the original problem gets solved, the effect of the old reaction can still leave us with residual stress. This secondary effect is also a problem and it needs to be addressed.

To calm down or eliminate stress, we have to reduce or let go of these reactions by bringing them into the light and discussing them. Fortunately, we are not equally impacted by each trigger and usually only one or two show up in present problems.

Triggers to Old Reactions

- Invasion of our territory or responsibilities
- Deadlines imposed by others
- Nonsupport from key people
- Being deprived of what we need or want
- Criticism of competency or integrity
- Failing and making mistakes
- Being blamed
- Unclear or excessive authority
- Contradictory expectations

- Win or lose, right or wrong competition
- Resistance and opposition
- Uncertainty and vague information
- Overload from too much work
- Non-communication or silent treatment

In my own case, the old reactions were triggered by Nonsupport from People and Invasion of Territory or Responsibilities. As I faced the event of a growing consulting practice, these old reactions increased my stress. I could no longer do everything myself.

Calling on colleagues to share projects and give me a helping hand was a double-edged sword. Arising from my old reactions were the questions, "Can I depend on them, or will they intrude and spoil my relationship with clients?" and "Will they take over some of the fun and functions that are important to me?"

When I identified these primary old reactions, I was able to reason more objectively and share my concerns with my colleagues. Having these fears put to rest, I could pay more attention to the business at hand and get the job done.

After identifying and facing these underlying old fears, my natural and professional curiosity led me to wonder, "How did I become so sensitive to Nonsupport from People and Invasion of My Territory?" Memories started to flood back.

My mother was an independent woman in the 1930s. She ran a business and raised me. She was a super woman before it was the norm for a woman to be so openly competent. I admired her courage to go it alone, but she was so preoccupied with our survival that I often felt she could not be there when I needed her.

Ironically, when she was more available, she seemed to become too involved in what I was doing. I interpreted her questions, interest, and suggestions as "invasion of my territory."

New Double Lane Stress Model

In the stress literature, there is strong emphasis on the medical consequences and the debilitating effects of burnout from stress. But notice in the Double Lane flow chart on the opposite page. "Burnout" and medical consequences in the negative lane are the very last and extreme position for stressful problems not tolerated, ignored, denied, or left unsolved. At this bottom, most negative position, the lane back to positive problem solving and raised tolerance is more difficult, to be sure.

But before such a downhill detour, we can confront stressful problems and stay in the positive lane by using the simple and easy to learn tolerance and solutions techniques. With stressful problems better tolerated and solved, the negative lane can be avoided.

We can feel stronger, more in control, proud of our increased mastery over stressful problems and stressful people. Health, happiness, and more productivity is the ultimate reward of the positive lane.

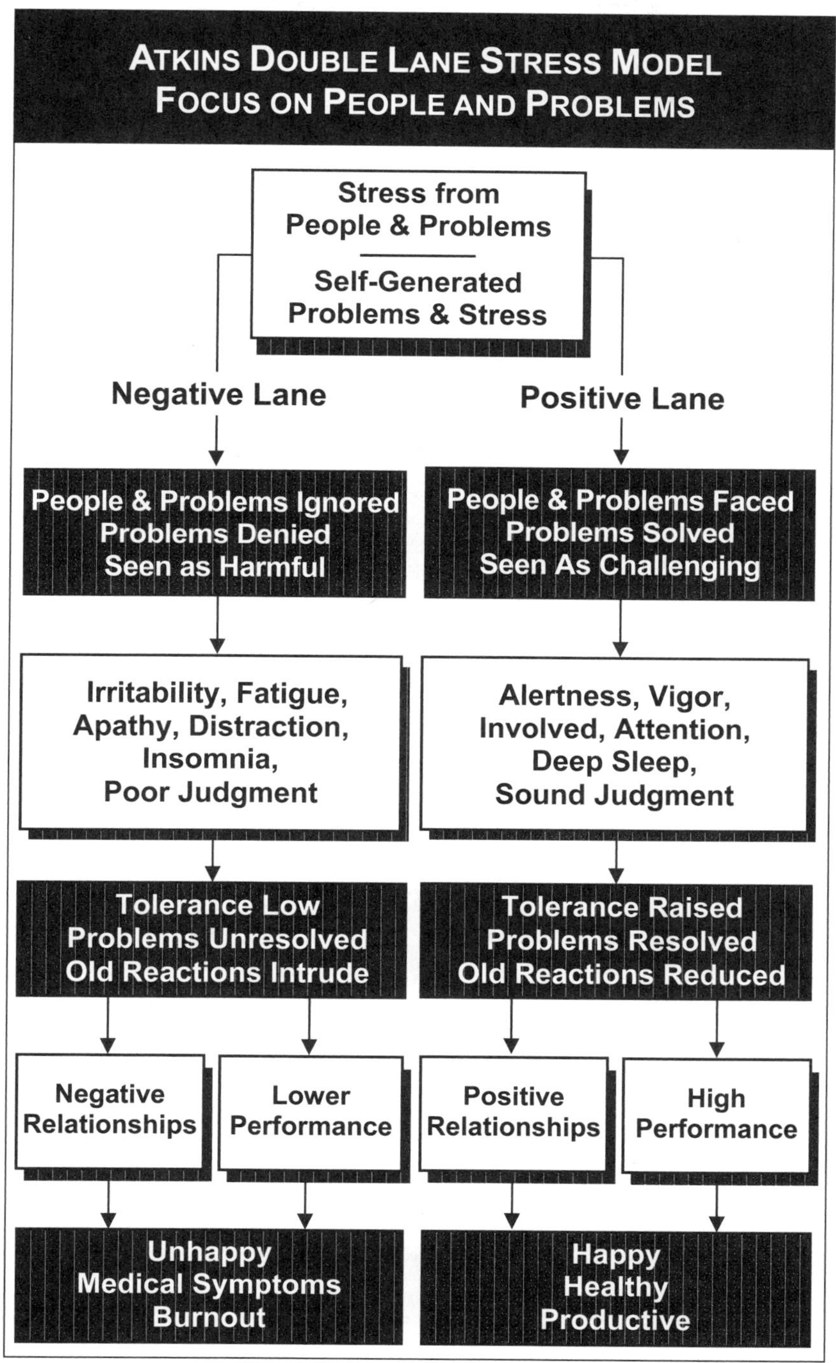
ATKINS DOUBLE LANE STRESS MODEL
FOCUS ON PEOPLE AND PROBLEMS
Stress from People & Problems
Self-Generated Problems & Stress
Negative Lane
Positive Lane
People & Problems Ignored
Problems Denied
Seen as Harmful
People & Problems Faced
Problems Solved
Seen As Challenging
Irritability, Fatigue, Apathy, Distraction, Insomnia, Poor Judgment
Alertness, Vigor, Involved, Attention, Deep Sleep, Sound Judgment
Tolerance Low
Problems Unresolved
Old Reactions Intrude
Tolerance Raised
Problems Resolved
Old Reactions Reduced
Negative Relationships
Lower Performance
Positive Relationships
High Performance
Unhappy
Medical Symptoms
Burnout
Happy
Healthy
Productive

CHAPTER 3

DISTRESS SIGNALS WHEN WE ARE FRUSTRATED OR UNHAPPY

Recognizing the Signals in What We Do

It was a star-filled sky on a warm, moonlit night and I was out at sea on my friend's sailboat. As the boat cut through the water, dark clouds began to drift across the moon. A strong breeze whipped across the bow, and the sea turned dark and rough. As my friend tried to control the boat, I began to realize that this might be too much for us.

In the distance, on the shoreline, I could see lights from the scattered buildings. Help seemed far away. I considered our options. We could shout for help, but we were far from shore. If it were daytime, we could wave our arms or twirl our jackets over our heads. If we had a flare gun, we could signal for help in the darkness, and if we had a radio, we could send out a Mayday signal with our exact position.

As quickly as the clouds drifted in, they drifted out. The moon was full again, lighting our way. The apparent danger had past.

Reflecting on this scare, I thought about how many signals there are to summon help in such physically dangerous situations. There are universal distress signals we all recognize. But in times of psychological danger, there are no such universal or standardized signals to communicate our need.

When we are "at sea" with problems in our daily lives and we can no longer "handle the boat," we feel out of control. That's when our usual way of acting "flares up" and the excesses of our behavior are clear for all to see.

Unfortunately, this excessive behavior is seldom recognized as a signal of distress or unhappiness. Yet when we begin to look and take notice, these signals are as visible and clear as an orange flare rocketing skyward.

Human distress signals are obvious when we say to ourselves, "Well, since our efforts are failing, or things seem out of control, or I'm afraid this or that will happen, why not use more effort, more of what works for us?" Then we reach into our reserve energy bank and put something extra into our efforts. The something extra is usually just more of the same thing but much more of it. Frequently, this doesn't help to solve the problem. It adds more stress by putting off other people. It also depletes our problem-solving energy and judgment.

Often, we are less rational and more emotional when our actions exceed what's productive. As a result, our behavior alienates other people, preventing them from recognizing and empathizing with our underlying stress and unhappiness.

Beyond Fight-Flight When We "See" Danger

Early stress researchers called our basic stress response to threats the fight or flight response. They said that when we face danger, we automatically go through a complex series of biochemical changes in the body that prepare us either to stay and fight or take off in flight.

That may have been so with prehistoric man or in the animal kingdom, but that is incomplete. In the face of danger, some of us stay around and fret, worry ourselves and others over and over about the same threat or problem. Others stay and frustrate themselves and others with analysis of the danger and many, many options to solve the problem—instead of solving it!

If we watch ourselves or others, we can tell how much stress is being experienced. Exaggerations or excesses of our behavior will indicate the degree to which stressful problems and people are impacting us. This exaggerated behavior will also tell us that we need to better tolerate the problem and, best of all, solve it.

Behavior That Signals We Are Stressed and Unhappy

Many of us do our better work under some stress. It's only when stress continues because of unresolved problems, and the goals of our behavior patterns are blocked, that stress leads to more trouble. Below are four universal behavioral patterns that men and women around the world use to live and work—and at times, under stress, come to exaggerate. And they sometimes create their own stress by being lured into excessive behavior because their patterns give them such great satisfaction.

If we have a **Controlling** pattern and emphasize action …

We can cope with stress effectively by being quick to respond with intensified effort. With a sense of urgency, we can deal with many problems on several fronts simultaneously. However, we run the risk of diffusing our efforts by running ourselves ragged and acting unilaterally instead of checking things out with the other people involved. Our urgency can exaggerate to emergency, throwing others into feeling pressured.

With stressful problems, we are likely to … FIGHT

Forced action is our central response.

Blaming others and getting defensive is another signal.

We …

- overemphasize disagreement, making it difficult for others to cope.
- make others feel defensive by being overly vigilant and combat ready.
- press people, not allowing them breathing room to decide.
- respond without checking policies or clearing with authorities.
- run ourselves ragged, often diffusing our effort.
- will not let others sufficiently advise us or be a resource.

If we have an **Adapting** pattern and focus on harmony …

We frequently handle stress by striving to keep tension low, getting things done through humor, and smoothing things out with reassuring promises and a positive outlook. The other side of this—the excess—is that we distract ourselves and others from the seriousness of the situation. Also, we may raise hopes too high, disappointing others if things don't work out.

With stressful problems, we signal by taking … FLIGHT

Avoiding trouble and sidestepping confrontation is the key.

Flip-flopping and over compromising is another signal.

We …

- appear so compromising that we create doubt about our true position.
- make light of trouble, diffusing its seriousness and creating a sense of artificial well-being.
- smooth over disagreement and prevent objections from being expressed so that problems recur.
- convey a lack of commitment or involvement by easy or uncontested agreement.
- divert attention from problems with jokes and playfulness.

If we have a **Supporting** pattern and strive for excellence …

We are willing to assume responsibility, to take the blame, and to try to do better by working harder or longer hours. While this often effectively copes with stress, it can also lead to the excess of becoming critical of ourselves and others when the impossible can't be achieved. When things are not going well, we say that it's up to us to do better. "Good" people should do it.

With Supporting, then, our signal is to … FRET

Worry underlies our actions.

Blaming ourselves for problems and giving in to people is another signal.

We …

- become critical of ourselves and others when we can't achieve the impossible.
- over rely on others for decisions when unsure.
- become self-denying and make many concessions.
- accept too many unreasonable demands.
- give in to opposition rather than be seen as uncooperative.
- become moralistic and convey injustice done to us.

If we have a **Conserving** pattern and value reason …

We cope with stress by analyzing alternatives and setting priorities in a level-headed way, approaching the problem systematically. If this becomes exaggerated to excess, analysis paralysis can set in, decision deadlines can be missed, and the hazards and urgency in the situation can be ignored, as if we have all the time in the world.

Under too much stress, we are likely to … FRUSTRATE self and others

A lack of flexibility predominates.

Withdrawing and becoming stubborn is another primary signal.

We …

- detach ourselves from the trouble, frustrating others from a lack of sustained effort.

- lock into analysis paralysis and fail to take decisive action.
- alienate people by not showing enough feeling and concern, appearing uninvolved.
- document our position with facts, overwhelming others with detail.
- refuse to budge when new solutions are recommended; we stick to old ways.
- intellectualize the problem and do not experience the urgency and the hazards.

These, then, are the four basic stress signals:

FIGHT

FLIGHT

FRET

FRUSTRATE

What is basic to all four, however, is … FRIGHT.

Fright is more fundamental and precedes the four stress responses to danger—real or imagined, physical or psychological.

Fright is the "boo!" when kids jump out of doorways and scare each other. It's the haunted house and ghosts in the dark. It's fright night on TV or like watching a horror movie. It is like the roller coaster ride on which we try to master our fright.

Fight, flight, fret, or frustrate follow the scare when we think we see danger.

If we pay attention to people's excessive behavior, we will be able to help them identify the events, people or old reactions that cause them to sense danger and then experience stress and unhappiness.

Unfortunately, we often see exaggerated behavior as just unacceptable and unproductive. We try to correct or punish the behavior in order to put a stop to it. However, this usually leads to more stress, defensiveness, negative feelings in the relationship, more unhappiness and lower personal productivity.

It's useless to punish a signal flare. That won't help the person "at sea" with their problems. What they need are problem-solving techniques and ways to tolerate problems while they are being solved, or ways to tolerate them if they cannot be solved at all.

Case History: The Unhappy Supervisor

In the long run, facing up to a stressful problem is easier than trying to reverse the consequences that come from avoiding a problem. In this case of the unhappy supervisor, we can observe the negative consequences at work and home of ignoring one's stress signals and the problems that are causing them.

The Stressful Event

David Martin is a store manager at Shopper's World, a small supermarket chain in the Midwest. Dave started out as a checker ten years ago and worked his way up. He was known as a consistently hard worker who always went out of his way to help customers and make sure they were being served properly.

Recently, there have been changes in his attitude. If a customer asks him a question, he sometimes gets impatient and tells them to talk to somebody else. The people he supervises used to think of him as an excellent boss, but now some of them complain that he doesn't treat them fairly. Also, some say they have to remind him several times to follow through when he says that he will do something.

A few months ago there was a reorganization at Shopper's World when it was bought by All Foods, a larger chain of supermarkets. Dave used to report to Sam Fillmore, the owner of Shopper's World. Now, in addition to Sam, he also reports to Leslie Jones, the new general manager of All Foods at the head office.

His old boss, Sam, places emphasis on quality customer service, and had been very pleased with Dave's overall performance. Leslie Jones, on the other hand, emphasizes keeping costs down. He has been hinting that David is too eager to please customers by giving refunds. What's more, some of the refunds are not within company policy. Leslie told Dave that he needs to make changes to conform to the policies of All Foods. Leslie also has been asking Dave for more detailed reports, which makes him think that Leslie mistrusts him. Dave finds himself working harder to please Leslie, but he isn't handling all the new policies well.

Dave's wife, Anne, has been noticing that he hasn't quite been himself. He comes home each day more tired than usual, and he yells at the children much more than he used to. For the first time in their eight-year marriage, he forgot her birthday. Anne also commented that he hasn't been sleeping well. He takes a long time to fall asleep, sleeps rather restlessly, and has a hard time waking up in the morning. He used to drink just one cup of coffee with breakfast, but now he drinks three cups.

One day Anne suggested to Dave that maybe he's working too hard. He immediately became defensive and shot back, "Well, I'm doing it for you and the kids!" Then, after thinking for a few moments, he said, "OK, maybe you have a point. But I'm sure it will pass. Right now things are just a little confused. I try to do what Sam and Leslie want, but there's just too much to do. I keep trying, because I don't want to let them down. I think they need to get their heads together. I'm not always sure they agree with each other. Oh, well, things will work out soon."

Analysis

As we can tell, Dave is experiencing the negative impact of too much stress. If he allows his situation to continue, he may move on in the stress lane to low performance and eventually long burnout.

Dave's basic behavior pattern is Supporting. Notice his loyalty to Sam, his old boss, while he tries his best for Leslie, his new boss. Because his pattern is Supporting, Dave's basic desires are to be seen as a responsible and worthwhile person, to be valued and trusted, and to maintain what he feels are high standards.

Also, Dave favors Adapting as a secondary pattern. He tries to please and is unnerved by the disagreement between his old boss and the new one. In this stressful situation, it is now difficult for him to be seen as likeable and as a person who can get along. His basic life pattern is being thwarted and disconfirmed. Expressing irritation at both customers and employees, Dave just adds more stress to fuel his existing problems.

Old Reactions

With Dave, there is one old reaction adding to his trouble. It is coming from his bosses' contradictory expectations pulling him in opposite directions. Another old reaction is from change happening too fast, creating feelings of being overloaded.

So Dave has his hands full, getting back to being a high performing and happier person. Time may be on his side. He may eventually be able to catch up with all the changes, but he needs to find a way to face Sam and Leslie and help them realize they have him "betwixt and between." If he is successful in this, they may try to be more consistent in their relationship because they realize how it impacts Dave's performance.

Prescription for Better Performance

To get Dave out of the stress lane, and back to better performance, reprimanding or complaining will not correct the source problems. Insisting that he stop being critical and impatient with customers and employees will do little good. These are the distress signals. It also is of little help if Dave emotionally scolds himself for being "bad." Nor does being scolded by his wife alleviate the problem.

Being ostracized or criticized doesn't change the source of his trouble. It would only add to his feelings of frustration and inadequacy, and lead to continued loss of productivity.

Drive at the source of the trouble, solve or better tolerate the relationship problem with the bosses and reduce the intrusion of the old reactions—then his stress and negative behavior would diminish or disappear.

Part II

How to Tolerate People

CHAPTER 4

TAKING STRESSFUL PEOPLE IN STRIDE

Why People Rub Us the Wrong Way

Friend or foe, people have at least one thing in common—annoying, sometimes intolerable, excessive behavior. This is a strange commonality, to be sure. But in fact, those behaviors are so stressful to us that, at times, lovers and spouses, coworkers and bosses, parents and children, seem foes not friends.

What is it about them that irritates, angers, and exasperates us? What is so intolerable? Why is it so difficult to overlook that offending behavior, even in the people we love?

Early in my life and career, I searched for the answers to those questions. During this time, I sensed something was missing in the way I looked at people both in my work and in my personal life. I wasn't sure why certain people rubbed me the wrong way, and I didn't know why some people pleased me more than others. More personally, I wasn't sure who I could love or who I could not, and why. All the existing tests and techniques of the behavioral sciences did not seem to give me any answers.

While I was doing work on sales psychology and teaching salespeople how to improve their customer relationships, I noticed that each salesperson had some specific characteristics that put people off and diminished the chance for a sale. At first, I could not recognize those characteristics, but I could see that the prospects or customers became defensive.

Later, I realized what these characteristics were: too pushy, too self-righteous, too thorough or too agreeable. I called them the four deadly sins of selling.

But the four characteristics I initially identified proved to be just a short list. Below is a more complete list of stressful characteristics.

Which of these characteristics in other people stress you the most?

Stressful Characteristics

- Compliant
- Impatient
- Arrogant
- Plodding
- Literal
- Sullen

- Dramatic
- Passive
- Domineering
- Gullible
- Coercive
- Impulsive
- Inconsistent
- Rigid
- Stubborn
- Impractical
- Self-denying
- Aimless
- Nit-picking
- Critical
- Manipulative
- Perfectionist
- Changeable
- Overcommitted
- Childlike
- Self-belittling
- Misleading
- Risk-taking
- Vacillating
- Overprotective
- Data-centered

In my sales workshops, I also asked salespeople to think about their customers and prospects in terms of stressful characteristics.

This generated lively discussions. It was if they had stored months or years of stress and suddenly could release their frustration.

Of course, I soon learned that the negative impact of these stressful characteristics was not the sole problem of salespeople. Managers, nurses, ministers, engineers, homemakers, accountants, and psychologists reacted in the same way. In fact, these alienating characteristics proved widespread in countries around the world!

Learning to accept the universality and inevitability of stressful characteristics will go a long way in helping us tolerate them.

Another way to better tolerate these stressful behaviors is to identify why we react so negatively to them. In general, the answer can be found in our earlier life experiences.

Why Stressful Characteristics Rub Us the Wrong Way

First, we may have been the target of those stressful behaviors, or just around them, and found them oppressive or extremely annoying. In my own case, I found that the people who liked to check and recheck my work and their own were very stressful to me. Any sustained inquiry annoyed me considerably. I wanted them to get on with the action.

This carried over to my work with a client organization in which all the key executives preferred to check and recheck issues and thoroughly study even the lowest priority matters. Meeting after meeting, they continuously wanted to fact-find and analyze. It was as if they were trying to engineer a risk-free future before they moved ahead. Their way of handling things irritated me. I found myself wondering, "Don't these people ever act spontaneously, shoot from the hip?"

Fortunately for me, the colleague with whom I was working understood their behavior and was quite comfortable with it. Through him, and my exposure to this group, I learned that quick decisions were less important to some people. More important to them was certainty and the satisfaction of a thorough analysis—twice!

I could see the benefits of more patience, thoroughness, and structure. But, oh, those factual, step by step explanations and explorations!

Why had these particular behaviors stressed me so? It didn't take long to figure it out. I remembered that while

I was growing up, my mother always needed to know where I was, what I was doing. I had to report. If not, she would inquire, "Where'd you go? Who'd you see? What'd you do?" She needed to be informed and have no surprises with unpredictable problems.

Even in her eighties, when she visited me in California, she needed to be on top of things. No sooner had her plane from Philadelphia arrived, and we had exchanged hugs and retrieved her luggage, when she would ask, "What's the plan for tomorrow? I'd like to see Aunt Janet on the following day. Then the next day we can go to a studio, and next I want to go to Disneyland. Do you have anything planned for next week? When we get to the house, let's call the airline and reconfirm my reservation back to Philadelphia."

As a boy, I had experienced my mother's behavior from her need for certainty as totally unnecessary and as investigative snooping.

I began to actively reject her way of doing things, even though there was an obvious strength in anticipating, getting information early on, and taking a more thorough, systematic approach to things.

Nevertheless, being the target of her stressful characteristics made me recoil from any semblance of that behavior. What's more, I had no friends who anticipated to that degree, or for that matter, who were that thorough or analytical.

After watching my more analytical clients in action, I realized that I needed to become more comfortable and less stressed by this behavior. It would be impractical, if not impossible, to avoid people with these characteristics.

I began to practice being more methodical and systematic. For example, on three-by-five cards, I wrote key phrases. One said, "Think now, act later," another, "Take a second look." Another said, "Opportunity knocks twice." A final card read, "You don't have to respond immediately—it won't go away."

Beside my desk near the telephone, I taped them on the wall as constant reminders. When a call came from a client, and I was asked to do a project, instead of responding immediately, I'd say, "Well, I need to talk this over with the staff," or, "Let me think more about it and call you back tomorrow." My surprise was that most clients did not mind being put off for awhile—if they thought their questions would be more thoroughly analyzed.

I learned to explore alternatives, to be more thorough and systematic. It felt like a grind at first. I thought I was plodding. I experienced this unfamiliar behavior as if I were using it to the extreme. But with my need for action there was no fear of getting stuck on dead center, or slowing down into analysis paralysis.

The second reason why we are stressed by certain behavior is that we are uncomfortable with the unfamiliar. Simply, this means that certain people's typical behavior is foreign to us. Here we are all living in the same country, working in the same organization and possibly doing identical work and we don't understand why certain people act the way they do! That inability to understand the reasons for their "strange" behavior creates confusion, mistrust and then stress.

Just gaining familiarity with why these people do things the way they do makes them understandable and more trustworthy. This understanding raises our tolerance and reduces our stress.

For example, one manager I know, Francine, enjoys being in charge, making most decisions entirely on her own. For her, it is exhilarating to take care of work with high-energy effort in quick, sustained bursts of accomplishment.

But other people who want to work more as a team and make group decisions, drive Francine "up the wall." She insists that these people are avoiding initiative and are afraid to act independently. What else could it be? she persists. My answer: How about the value of building on each others' ideas for more complete and committed solutions to problems. But this group behavior is unfamiliar to her. Most of her past positions only required such solo effort.

Looking back through Francine's history, she was encouraged to act alone and be considered suspect if she asked for help. Everyone in her family had their own "claim to fame." She was in statewide competition as a debater. Her sister was active in swimming competitions. Mother played golf and father was club champ in singles tennis. Her two brothers were track and field competitors, one competing in the mile event, the other in the high jump.

Practice sessions and events had them running off in separate directions all week. At Sunday dinner they each shared their individual exploits of the week. They all respected each other's efforts and, schedule permitting, they tried to attend as many of each other's events as possible.

While they were a close family, giving each other encouragement and support, they had little experience in collaboration on a mutual problem. If they had a problem, they were left to solve it on their own. Togetherness came on Sunday when individual accomplishments were shared.

In later years at work, she found more group-oriented activities difficult. She became impatient with people who were reluctant to move quickly and who desired more collaboration. She believed that they were too dependent or lazy and should be encouraged to act more independently. After a time, her stress with these people became a source of discomfort, and she distanced herself from them when she could.

After she became aware of the reasons for her stress with these people, she took some time to understand the value of collaboration. Moreover, she even began to appreciate their satisfactions from working together on a team.

While their behavior became less stressful to her, she still expected them to be independent and work out their problems. Being less stressed about it, she did not seem impatient and disappointed with them. It helped their morale and made them want to meet her expectations. She is still the model of self-sufficiency and independent action. Her people are learning self-sufficiency from her, and she is learning collaboration from them—reluctantly, but with just occasional twinges of stress.

The third reason certain behavior creates a stressful reaction is that in our earlier experience it was unacceptable, even punishable.

Carl grew up in a well-organized family with traditions, rules, and regulations. If he tried to be informal and do things expediently, going outside of the standard rules of the family, he would hear about it in no uncertain terms. Kidding around was judged as frivolous and childish. It was acceptable to laugh—as long as you did not make a habit of it!

When Carl went to college away from home, he was uncomfortable with dorm life, its high social interaction and its informality. If other students broke the rules, he would become stressed. To no one's surprise, his unwillingness to circumvent the rules did not make him popular, nor did his parental attitude and preachments about following the rules.

Later in his career, he was very successful as an audit supervisor in a financial services company. Helping department heads in client organizations was his primary responsibility. He assisted them in developing better financial controls. His duties were twofold: investigative and educational.

His team of five auditors was seen as the financial police, trying to catch financial sloppiness or wrongdoing. However, that was not their intention—to be seen only as investigative. They wanted to train department heads to become more financially astute in order to cut costs.

In part, this suspicious view of the auditors was due to the nature of their role. But the other part involved Carl's difficulty in tolerating a friendly and light touch by his team. His insistence on a serious approach—even somber, made it difficult to win the trust and confidence of department heads in the organization.

Though Carl and his audit team had been together for five years, their meetings were never fun or zestful. Carl would get upset if they became too loose by telling jokes or ribbing each other. This was too close to his family's taboo on levity. Seriousness and nothing but seriousness was acceptable. If not, he experienced his parents' displeasure which was punishment enough to bring him in line.

Later in life, when somebody started to joke around, his stress was triggered—instantly. Of course, after he encountered this stress-inducing behavior, he gave his standard lecture and preachment about the need to be serious and stay focused.

Despite his avowed desire to have his group's approach be educational, his stressful reactions to "lighter" behavior discouraged it. Instead, his sometimes chilling formality played into the policeman perception.

To help Carl see the contradiction between his goal and his behavior, I began by inquiring about which characteristics were most stressful to him. We discussed how this came to be, and the trade-offs between formality and informality. Understanding how informality and the light touch can help develop rapport and trust, he slowly experimented with informality, allowing his audit team greater latitude with that behavior.

In a short time, he was able to feel less stressed in the presence of that informality. At a much later time, he tried some of that behavior himself, but not too comfortably. He decided it was not really him, but it was okay for others if they chose.

That is how it goes when we try to take our stressful people in stride—a step at a time, gradually raising our tolerance. Eventually, we can allow others their behavior by understanding the source of our stressful reaction and developing a "live and let live" attitude.

To reduce our stress, we need only follow these few steps. First, we have to identify the particular characteristics that are stressful to us.

Second, we have to understand that those characteristics are either excessive, unfamiliar behavior, or just ways of doing things in which we place little value.

Third, we must accept the universality and the inevitability of excessive behavior, and that the stressful person is not unique in their behavior and, in most cases, is not deliberately making us "miserable."

Fourth, if we want to further reduce our stress from this behavior, we need to understand the earlier situations in which we encountered the behavior.

And, finally, to complete our understanding and quiet our stress, it is helpful to know 1) if, in our early development, we were the target of some significant person's similar excessive characteristics, or 2) was this kind of behavior not present in our early experience so that we became uncomfortable with the unfamiliar, or 3) was this behavior in our younger life unacceptable, even punishable?

Quietly, imperceptibly, people slip beyond their productive behavior into excess. They unknowingly do too much of a good thing. Their stress pushes them there. Or, in pursuit of more satisfactions and personal gratification, they go overboard trying too hard to feed their pattern gluttony.

As an organizational consultant, frequently I would interview people's coworkers and bosses. In my interviews, they would describe a person as too pushy but also persistent and someone who took initiative and got things done. The person whose "bad habit" was described as too self-righteous was also described by many as someone who had high standards and was very principled, who really kept them doing their very best work. Now, when I discussed the person who slowed down the work flow by being too thorough, many coworkers also had nothing but praise for how well the person was organized and how carefully they did their work. Finally, the person who was described as too agreeable or wishy-washy, was also seen as cooperative and flexible, someone who kept peace and harmony between people.

It seemed as if the coworkers were describing two different people, or they could not make up their mind. I wondered which description was the accurate one. Was it assertive or too pushy, principled or too self-righteous, careful or too thorough, cooperative or too agreeable?

I finally realized and confirmed what I had been observing. Both observations about people were accurate, even though they seemed contradictory. It wasn't either/or, it was simply a behavior and its extreme extension. The very same thing that made people as successful as they were was also the very same thing that was getting them criticism! They had merely exaggerated their strong points, used their positive characteristics so much that they turned into "weaknesses." It was too much of a good thing. Since these negative characteristics derived from the overuse of their strengths, I called them excessive strengths or excesses, not bad habits or weaknesses.

If we view a person's exaggerated and displeasing behavior as a self-contained and unconnected action rather than connected to their productive behavior which pleases us, then it is easy to judge them as inept or impossible. But if we can understand that behind those negative behaviors is something we value, then what might be annoying or intolerable is something we can live with. "Love me, love my excesses!" is the declaration that should be made. "You just can't have my strengths without my excesses—they're attached, part of the same package."

Below is a list of negative behaviors and the positive source from which they stem. Behavior, indeed, is not a bag of unconnected and unrelated behaviors.

Positive Source of Negative Behavior

Negative Behavior	**Positive Source**
Self-effacing	Modest
Overprotective	Helpful
Gullible	Trusting
Passive	Cooperative
Domineering	Directing
Impatient	Active
Arrogant	Confident
Impulsive	Quick
Data-bound	Factual
Complicated	Systematic
Plodding	Methodical
Stingy	Thrifty
Wishy-washy	Accommodating
Aimless	Flexible
Flamboyant	Enthusiastic
Placating	Tactful

We all would like the positive behavior without the negative. Unless we give up that wish, we are destined for disappointment and stress. Our wishful thinking makes us have unrealistic expectations for the other person and our wish goes unfulfilled.

Letting go the unrealistic expectation will help us tolerate the excess and live with it more comfortably. And ending a relationship or removing someone from a situation may temporarily remove one set of excesses, but there will be another set of excesses with the new person. Perhaps their excesses will be less annoying, but then again the excesses may be equally exasperating, if not more.

Stuck on the Negative

Having connected the negative behavior to the positive, and having taken the position that behavior is really on a sliding scale from positive to negative, unfortunately some people get stuck at the negative end. Either their unresolved stressful problems have them temporarily stuck or the stress has been going on for so many years that their negative behavior has become their customary response to most situations and most people.

Most of us, however, are not stuck on the negative, and can move along the sliding scale back to the positive after we solve our stressful problem or tolerate the stressful person.

Searching for the Middle Ground

To further study degrees of human behavior, I examined dictionaries. They were filled with adjectives that described hundreds of characteristics, but they were alphabetically scattered throughout. When I first searched for words to describe human behavior by degrees, from positive to negative, I could not find terms to describe the phenomenon. I found only either/or: trusting or gullible, quick or impulsive, methodical or plodding, flexible or acquiescent.

Where were the words to describe us between those extremes, words that might give us clues or warning signals that we are approaching the excess, the negative? At first examination, there was only right or wrong, good or bad, strong or weak. This polar thinking, I realized, prevents us from seeing how our actions are a matter of degree, more or less, a position between two poles.

Finally, I did find some words that described the middle ground between strength and excess, the positive and negative. I have listed them in the table below to give us a signal that we are about to do too much, and we may be being pushed by stress over the threshold into negative behavior.

3 Stages of Behavior

1 **Positive** **Just Right**	2 **Warning** **Threshold**	3 **Negative** **Too Much**
Caring	Indulging	Over-protective
Idealistic	Impractical	Utopian
Modest	Deferring	Self-effacing
Trusting	Guileless	Gullible
Loyal	Devoted	Blind Faith
Cooperative	Compliant	Passive
Helpful	Overcommitted	Overwhelmed
Confident	Cocky	Arrogant
Forceful	Insistent	Coercive

3 Stages of Behavior (cont'd)

1 **Positive** **Just Right**	2 **Warning** **Threshold**	3 **Negative** **Too Much**
Quick	Scattered	Impulsive
Competitive	Contentious	Combative
Sparing	Stingy	Miserly
Reserved	Aloof	Withdrawn
Practical	Utilitarian	Unimaginative
Systematic	Elaborate	Complicated
Factual	Concrete	Data-bound
Tactful	Solicitous	Placating
Enthusiastic	Excitable	Flamboyant
Humorous	Silly	Foolish
Negotiating	Vacillating	Yielding
Experimental	Drifting	Aimless
Flexible	Impressionable	Acquiescent
Eager	Flighty	Childish

Accepting that the connection between positive and negative behavior as a fact of life, we can better tolerate this irony of human nature. If, however, we want to take the next step, help ourselves and others stop the behavior at the early warning stage, we can give and receive constructive feedback.

We can prevent ourselves from crossing the threshold into excess, either because we are overdoing a good thing to signal that we need help from stressful people and problems, or we are pushing our actions to the extreme for our own pleasure.

The question then arises, how can you tell if the behavior is just overdoing for self-satisfaction or a signal of stress?

Like language, words have different meanings according to the context in which they are used. What's behind the excess behavior—pleasure or pain—makes its intent clear depending upon the situation in which it is happening.

It is usually apparent when the situation is stressful. There is visible intensity, and we can sense the trouble. When the excess is pleasure-based, the situation is usually less hectic and the person has time for excessive self-satisfaction.

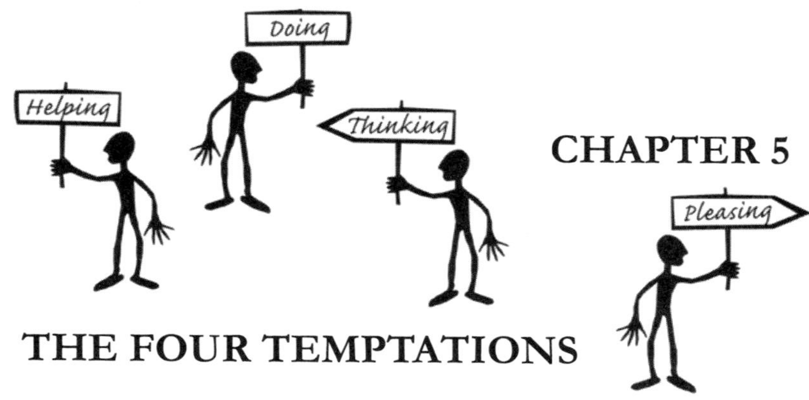

CHAPTER 5

THE FOUR TEMPTATIONS

Self-Generated Problems and Stress

While tolerating the outside sources of problems and stress is important, equally important—and sometimes easier to control—are self-generated problems and stress. Within a section of Chapter 2, I introduced to you what underlies this—the Four Temptations. Remember them?

HELPING: Giving our all with high standards, trying to be a worthy and helpful person.

DOING: Taking what we need to get quick results and moving on to the next challenge.

THINKING: Holding on to what works and planning future effort a step at a time with facts and figures.

PLEASING: Dealing and compromising to keep things running smoothly and influencing with a light touch.

For example, the pleasure in our patterns may lead us to seek responsibility and work harder than others to meet our high standards, while helping others to do the same. Or, we can get quick results with a challenging project never done before, rallying and directing people to get behind it. Some of us get pleasure from laying out a plan with alternatives based on what worked well before, and with a timetable for each step of the way. Others may find pleasure in smoothing over tense situations with a light touch and finding ways for everyone to compromise, especially when all are pleased with the solution and us.

Those are some of our tempting pleasures. That's us. We love it! Therefore, why not do as much of it as possible? It's so confirming and pleasurable.

Ah, but gluttony is our undoing. As we have seen in a previous chapter, there can be too much of a good thing. Our pleasure can be someone else's displeasure. Others can sense the self-serving nature of our efforts and feel put upon, and react negatively to stop us.

What's more, perhaps the task at hand does not require so much hard work, quick action, extensive analysis, or that much compromise. What comes naturally to us may not be what is naturally required in a particular situation. Nevertheless, we pour our time and energy into it, often letting other projects pile up. But because our favorite patterns give us such pleasure, we don't think twice about whether our actions can lead to overload and stress.

Pleasure wins out.

We have created stress by reducing the time we have for our many other pressing responsibilities. Underlying time management is managing the temptations.

'Supporting' Temptations

With this pattern, it is important to remember that pleasure comes from hard work and seeking excellence.

It also comes from being thoughtful, trusting, idealistic, and loyal. People with this pattern try to do their very best and set high standards for themselves and others.

When overdone, the person with a supporting pattern can become trapped in the pursuit of perfection. Practical standards, however, clearly indicate that what is already accomplished is acceptable. The situation does not warrant more effort. To give it more is like being on a treadmill—much exercise but going nowhere. Trying harder may be a waste of effort if new thinking is required. In some cases, it might be better to work smarter, not harder.

With the supporting pattern, we also can be delighted at any opportunity to help someone in need. We can be happy trying to make things right when they go wrong. At the slightest sign of someone's need, we can jump to rescue them.

While these inclinations are admirable and pleasurable, we can become overcommitted helping others. As a result, we can neglect our own needs, and neglect the needs of other people who should be our priority.

Instead of taking so much responsibility, we need to think about who else should share the responsibility and let go the stressful pleasure.

'Controlling' Temptations

With controlling, the pleasure goal is realized by seizing opportunity, showing how competent we are, and getting quick results, even on the most difficult task. Pleasure also comes from making things happen by taking charge, being confident, and persuasive.

But we can be so captivated by the challenge of a difficult situation that we persist just to prove we can master and overcome the difficulty. Say it can't be done, and we'll show you it can. Overcoming is the pleasure, showing ourselves and others we can do it. We feel powerful. But we can overlook the time, effort and money it may have cost to get the results. We absorb the stress because the pleasure can mask the pain.

At the other extreme from difficult tasks, trivial tasks are also taken on just because they are there and require some action. It may be an inconsequential effort in the scheme of things but there is pleasure in the doing. For the sake of pleasure, we wind up overdoing, and running ourselves ragged. Trying to do too much too fast is sure to result in stress.

'Conserving' Temptations

Pleasure comes from being methodical, logical, precise, and tenacious. Before acting, we try to analyze every angle, always look for the fail-safe way to do a job. We enjoy the tried and true, the practical, making the most of what we have.

With Conserving, the pleasure of being right and accurate makes precision and completeness very important. When this is self-serving, it can lead to analysis paralysis, over elaborate planning and the overuse of information. Asked for the time of day, we'll give you a lecture on how a watch works.

Meanwhile, precious time is lost and tasks pile up waiting to be completed. This lack of closure is a source of stress.

Because we get such pleasure from making the most from existing resources, we may hold on to things that are well used and worn. In those cases, others can be stressed waiting to move on with the new, and we can be stressed when things need repair or just stop running, disrupting our schedule.

'Adapting' Temptations

With flexibility, enthusiasm, and tactfulness, people characterized by this Adapting pattern find pleasure in getting along with others. Those of us who have this pattern are pleased by pleasing, keeping events and relationships running smoothly. Getting to know people, therefore, and being aware of their needs and wants, helps us to facilitate them in getting what they want.

Often this leads us to ignore our own needs until we help others fill their needs first. If we are not careful, the pleasure of getting along can create the stress of continually placating others at our own expense.

Along with facilitating other people comes an unstated expectation. "Now that I have helped you get what you want, the bargain is that you must allow me to do what I want." If this private expectation is not realized, the stress from resentment can take over.

If we are involved in a significant situation with a number of people, we may find ourselves being pulled in different directions at the same time, particularly when they meet as a group. Trying to please everybody leads to stress. Stress heightens when we do not know whom we might offend by saying the "wrong" thing.

So there are the four temptations—in a word, helping, doing, thinking and pleasing.

These are all positive contributions to others and a pleasure to us—except when we overdo them.

But this is not a dead end. We can learn over a period of time how much pattern pleasure is enough, so that other people are not frustrated with us, and so we don't sacrifice effectiveness for undue satisfaction.

Breaking Free From Temptations

How do we deny ourselves pleasure? First, we need to redefine the situation. It has nothing to do with depriving ourselves. It has everything to do with seeing the situation as a chance to get pleasure without the pain of self-induced stress

This means learning to see the "line in the sand" where the next step means that we have crossed over into the territory of pain for pleasure.

Pleasure But Not Too Much—Just Right

Let's refer back to the idea of the quantitative view of our actions—the three stages: just right, early warning and too much. As described in Chapter 4, when I first searched for words to describe human behavior by degrees, from positive to negative, I could not find terms to describe the phenomenon. All that was obvious was either/or comparisons: trusting or gullible, quick or impulsive, methodical or plodding, flexible or aimless.

Where were the words to describe us between the extremes, words that might give us clues or warning signals that we are approaching the "too much" that can become stressful? Finally, I did find some words that described the middle ground between just right and stressful. They're here in the table below.

First, choose which category is most like you—supporting, controlling, conserving, or adapting. You may choose a second category if the single choice is difficult. Then select the individual behaviors in the category that tempt you the most.

The 1, 2, 3 of Self-Generated Stress

1 **Positive** **Just Right**	2 **Middle Ground** **Threshold**	3 **Stressful** **Too Much**
'SUPPORTING' TEMPTATIONS		
Caring	Indulging	Overprotective
Idealistic	Impractical	Utopian
Modest	Deferring	Self-effacing
Trusting	Guileless	Gullible
Loyal	Devoted	Blind Faith
Helpful	Overcommitted	Overwhelmed
'CONTROLLING' TEMPTATIONS		
Confident	Cocky	Arrogant
Forceful	Insistent	Coercive
Quick	Scattered	Impulsive
Competitive	Contentious	Combative
Directing	Bossy	Domineering
Urgent	Impatient	Demanding
'CONSERVING' TEMPTATIONS		
Methodical	Painstaking	Plodding
Sparing	Stingy	Miserly
Reserved	Aloof	Withdrawn
Practical	Utilitarian	Unimaginative
Systematic	Elaborate	Complicated
Factual	Concrete	Data-bound

'ADAPTING' TEMPTATIONS

Tactful	Solicitous.................	Placating
Enthusiastic	Excitable	Flamboyant
Humorous	Silly...........................	Foolish
Negotiating.........	Vacillating...............	Yielding
Experimental......	Drifting	Aimless
Flexible................	Impressionable.......	Acquiescent

The connection between positive and negative behavior is a fact of life, and we can better tolerate this irony of human nature if we accept it. If we want to take the next step, help ourselves and others stop behavior at the early warning stage (column 2), we can by alerting each other caringly with constructive feedback.

Affirm and Guide Technique

The first step in constructive feedback is acknowledging the positive behavior from which the negative stems. After appreciating our positive actions, we can then make specific recommendations for more productive action. These guidelines can lead us back from self-induced stress or prevent us from slipping into it.

Here are four life situations, one for each behavior pattern, illustrating the Affirm and Guide technique.

Controlling Pattern

Diane is meeting with her partner Phyllis. They are evaluating different brands of furniture for their new offices. Phyllis is explaining some of the details of the modular system she has researched. There are several more catalogs on her desk which she plans to present to Diane in just a few minutes.

Diane reaches over Phyllis's desk and picks up a catalog and starts scanning through it. She says, "Hey, these conference tables look really great. We should buy these. Here's the toll free number. Let's find out the delivery time on these." (Hasty—early warning for Impulsive, a stress-producing behavior.)

Phyllis, says, "You know I admire how quickly you make a decision, Diane. (Affirmative feedback). But why don't we consider at least one more option? We need to be sure to get the best value on our limited budget. I'll check on the delivery." (Guide to action)

Diane pauses for a moment and says, "Okay. But let's do it fast. Delivery could be four to six weeks."

If Phyllis had become bothered by Diane reaching over her desk and hastily grabbing a catalog, the situation could have changed. As Diane reached across the desk before Phyllis finished her presentation, Phyllis could have said, "Hey, Diane. You never let me finish. I'm not sure about those conference tables."

Diane responds sarcastically, "We could work on orange crates if you like." She reaches for the telephone.

Phyllis puts her hand on the receiver first. "Now hold on, Diane. I can't let you make another impulsive decision. Remember how you rushed into buying our computer?"

As you can see, this could lead to hard feelings and a stressful situation. But if they followed the first scenario, conflict could be avoided by affirming Diane's quickness and guiding her toward productive action, rather than making it personal.

Supporting Pattern

Bill is working on an information packet that will be used by five volunteers in a phone campaign to invite people to a political meeting and fund-raising campaign. It is 10 o'clock on a Tuesday evening and he is using the family home computer to complete his third draft.

He is pleased with how it reads, but he doesn't feel it is the best he can do. He wants to do another draft to make it even better. (Early Warning Signal—Meticulous leading to Negative Behavior—Perfectionist) His wife, Doris, notices his sigh of dissatisfaction. She comes over, looks over his shoulder at the draft and says, "You've really worked hard on these projects. It looks great." (Affirmation)

She gently massages his shoulders. "You've done the very best job possible with the time available to you. Honey, it may not be perfect, but it's really good. (Affirmation). Wouldn't you like to get some sleep now so you can do your best in the meeting with the volunteers in the morning?" (Guide toward Productive Action) He takes a deep breath, sighs and is silent for a moment. "All right," he says, "I suppose you're right. It's probably good enough the way it is."

Now this scene easily could have caused more stress for Bill. Suppose Doris felt ignored because Bill had been working late at the computer. If she wanted to express her irritation, she could have walked over to him and said, "Look, Bill, you've done three drafts already. If it isn't right by now, it never will be. You're wasting your time, and mine. Besides, you don't even get paid for it."

The way their stress will go is clearly under their control. If statements about Bill's temptations and negative behavior are the focus of the discussion, if the positive behavior behind his negative action is not acknowledged and appreciated, and if productive action is not recommended, then it is argument time between Bill and his wife with stress, anger, and hurt feelings to follow.

Generally, self-induced stress, goodwill, and affection are under our control. Being stress-free is possible through the means of affirmative feedback with guiding recommendations. These constructive feedback skills are simple to learn and easy to apply.

Conserving Pattern

In another situation, Helen has been analyzing three different locations for the company's year-end sales meeting. She has written the Chamber of Commerce in each place and gathered all the information about things to do, places to go and hotel facilities.

She has developed a filing system for all the brochures and flyers, and she has written down the pluses and minuses of each place on separate pieces of paper. In order to make a decision, she has also compiled a list of all the things everyone on the committee wants from the location. She is now evaluating each alternative accordingly.

Her co-chairperson, John, comes into her office. "You know, I've been thinking," says Helen. "We need a little more information to make our final decision." (Early Warning Signal—Elaborate leading to Negative Behavior—Complicated) "Really?" asks John, "What more do we need?" Helen answers, "Well, we haven't got enough information about the cost of the restaurants."

He looks at all the lists and brochures on Helen's desk for a moment and says, "Helen, I think it's great how systematically you go about this. I'm sure with your careful analysis whatever we decide will be fine. We won't have to worry about the sales group being disappointed after we get there (Affirmative Feedback). What do you think—let's decide today, so we can take the next step and actually plan the meeting." (Guide toward Productive Action).

Helen frowns for a moment and gets up from her desk. "Actually plan, huh. Good idea," she responds.

John's feedback was constructive, but it could have gone differently. He could have approached Helen in a way that would have created defensiveness and stress.

Going into Helen's office, John says, "Helen are you still at it?" He picks up some brochures, opens and closes them and drops them on her desk.

"Yes, John, but I need a little more information."

"You've got to be kidding! You're making it too complicated. By the time we go through the information, it will be time for the meeting." He turns to leave the office.

"Wait a minute, John. We have these meetings once a year. I'm not going to plunge ahead like you—blindly, then be disappointed when we get there."

And so the stress and mutual judgment mount, stemming from Helen's analytical satisfactions gone overboard, complicating her decision-making and her relationship with John.

Now let's consider another situation and different behavior.

Adapting Pattern

Dan is excited about the upcoming departmental awards dinner. He has been enthusiastically organizing the dinner for the past two months. He is in the middle of his morning coffee break, visiting with Sam and talking about the dinner.

Sam asks, "Did you hear about Hank and Betty? They're disappointed about missing the dinner. I heard they might be available the week after."

Dan replies, "Maybe we should postpone the dinner? I could call everybody and try to work it out. It would take some involved rearranging." (Changeable—Early Warning Signal leading to stress-inducing Disruptive)

Dan's boss, George, overhears the conversation. "Dan, I appreciate your being so flexible, and I know how you try to keep peace in the department (Affirmation), but changing now can really disrupt things. You have a lot of demands on your time already. Why not try to convince Hank and Betty to make a special effort to change their schedule (Guide to productive action)

"I can do that. Or maybe we'll just have to go ahead without them. They had plenty of notice."

Suppose Dan's boss is under the gun with some tough deadlines. The thought of Dan spending more of his time with the awards dinner is just too much.

The boss could exclaim, "Reschedule the awards dinner? You've got to be kidding!"

Dan looks dumbfounded. "Is there something wrong?" The boss snaps, "Wrong? It's a waste of time, that's what's wrong! You've got your priorities out of whack. Stop worrying about what other people think. The date stays!"

Muttering to himself, Dan is deflated. "Next year let him do it himself. Who needs it? Some thanks for all the work I did on my own time."

If Affirm and Guide works so well to keep people from going into stressful behavior, why don't we use it more often? The answer is that it feels good to express our frustration when people's temptations, their self-serving behavior, has a high impact on us. That's what the criticism and judgment do for us. They purge our frustration. But they don't correct the situation. Negative action begets a negative reaction. If we want a positive result with another person, we need a positive action.

At first consideration, affirmative feedback and guides toward productive action seem like the old "sandwich technique"—tell them something good before you tell them something bad and keep alternating.

That's not it. The old sandwich technique doesn't connect the negative behavior to its source—the person's positive actions and what they value in themselves. This is a key difference. Affirmation goes to the core of the person, his or her valued pattern, how they need to be seen and regarded by themselves and other people.

Again, we have a choice in stopping self-induced stress in ourselves and other people. We can vent our frustrations with punitive feedback or we can stop the behavior before it starts, at the early warning stage. By realizing that there are three stages to our behavior, we can begin to think of "how much" of a good thing is enough.

Thinking about "how much" gets us away from the dead end of the either/or dilemma which leads to right or wrong, good or bad, strong or weak. That's two-stage thinking.

What can liberate us from the either/or is three-stage thinking: Stage 1, positive core behavior reflecting one's values and successes; Stage 2, slight overuse of the positive behavior as an early warning signal; Stage 3, stress-producing overuse of positive behavior with negative impact on others.

Whether we criticize ourselves or others, or whether others do the same, it's often the self-satisfying, exaggerated behavior that's the target. Unfortunately, our first tendency is to change or stop the positive, core behavior instead of the just stopping the negative exaggerations. We try to throw out the positive behavior along with the negative exaggeration of it.

Giving up the positive source of the negative behavior is a high price to pay to stop stress. It's unnecessary. And it may create stress of its own. It is unproductive to give up what makes us as successful as we are. We should say, "Love me, love my negative exaggerations. They come from the best part of me."

Notwithstanding this call for acceptance of "too much of a good thing," we can learn to gear back from self-generated stress, and help others do the same, with feedback—providing it affirms us and guides us to productive action.

Part III

How to Tolerate Problems

CHAPTER 6

TOLERATING PERPLEXING PROBLEMS

Tolerance Techniques in Action

A new manager, Jackie, whom I helped hire into a client organization, relocated from the East Coast to the West Coast. Jackie's new boss, Gary, had promised her a senior accounts position, but until Jackie became oriented to the organization, Gary wanted her to work with junior accounts. Temporarily, she would be working for Helen, the junior accounts supervisor.

After several weeks on the job, Jackie told me in a follow up interview that she had become concerned. Gary had made himself scarce, while Helen gave her assignments beyond what should suffice as an orientation. It seemed like she had appropriated Jackie for her own department.

Nevertheless, Jackie mentioned to me that whenever she could, she introduced herself to some of the senior accounts people with whom she would eventually work. She wanted to learn from them more about the senior accounts job for which she was hired, and the more she learned, the more she became excited. "Now that's more like it," she said to me, "Those accounts are a challenge, and I can really show what I can do."

But after a month and a half, Jackie was still handling junior accounts. She told me that it was obvious to her what was going on. The company wanted her for junior accounts all along but made her the promise of senior accounts just to get her to come to work for them.

"No, wait a minute," she said, changing her mind. "It's Helen. She's smart. She wants to use my experience in her department, and she doesn't care if that delays my moving up in the organization.

"Doesn't my boss see what's happening?" Jackie asked with a look of disbelief.

"Maybe Helen persuaded Gary that I'm a better deal for the company in her department ... Worse, suppose she convinced him I'm not ready for senior accounts!" For a moment Jackie looked uncomfortable. "On second thought, who wants to work with a boss who can be so easily influenced?"

Then Jackie became angry. Nobody was going to pull that underhanded stuff on her! Suddenly a pang of doubt seemed to shoot through her. "Maybe this was a mistake," she concluded. "Maybe I should start looking around … Maybe I should call my former boss. See how things are going."

Jackie looked stressed. I noticed her shoulders pulled upward.

She looked tense. So I said, "Your new job is getting to you. Give the company a chance."

Jackie's response was defensive—like I doubted her judgment. "Give them a chance? You're kidding. Isn't a month and a half a good chance?"

"Three months is more reasonable", I noted. "You could be premature in your conclusion. At the moment, your boss just might have other priorities. He's under pressure, too."

Still defensive and puzzled Jackie allowed, "I guess you have to take their side. But I'm an important priority, too. They have a responsibility to me, even though I'm the new kid on the block. The pressure is on me to prove myself."

I realized that my rational viewpoint and rush to reality only aggravated Jackie's stress. It didn't help her calm down or think more clearly. I reminded myself of one of my tolerance techniques, an "anti-inflammatory," something to calm her down, not inflame her stress. She needed someone to hear her woes before trying to get her to fix the problem. She needed consoling first.

Consolation—Misery Loves Company

With consolation, I tried to convey more clearly that I was a sympathetic ally. I said to Jackie, "It's tough getting started. And that supervisor of junior accounts! She seems to have overlooked your feelings in the situation. And your boss, it would help if he realized that you're overdue."

"Overdue. I'm overcooked," Jackie added. "I'm boiling."

I continued my consolation. "They seem to have questionable judgment on this one. Here you are raring to go, hungry to show them what you can do, and they've got you locked in at the starting gate.

Jackie grinned and agreed, "Yes, that's exactly right."

With a tone of playfulness, I went on, "You know what I'd like to do? I'd like to call your boss and tell him, 'You can't do this to Jackie. She's moved here from back East, gave up a good job for what she thought would be a better one, and she's knocked herself out for a month and a half on junior accounts. How long does she have to wait before you let her do her best work?'"

Jackie laughed and I could feel her tension ease. "Oh, sure, you call my boss. Yes, I can just hear that. My boss says, 'Yes, sir, I'll get right on it'."

"OK. I just want you to know that I'm on your side, too."

"I appreciate that," Jackie said, reassuring me. "But don't worry. I can fight my own battles."

Teasing me, and giving me a dose of my own medicine, she joked, "Besides, it's only been a month and a half since I started the job. You know, you have to learn to be more patient!"

Having an ally seemed to restore Jackie's sense of the reality in the situation. By consoling, I did not create more frustration and stress. Nor did I encourage her discontent by asking her to use a quick fix to resolve her problem. To the contrary, first I gave Jackie a chance to blow off steam and reduce the stress. With less stress, she had more tolerance and a better chance for clear thinking.

In my experience, people with a stressful problem do not want it fixed right away. They are not ready for the facts until the emotion subsides.

Consolation is the first step in encouraging less emotion and more tolerance. It helps people to get the problem off their chest in uninterrupted waves of woe. By briefly lamenting and finding someone who will endure their lament, they can begin to see holes in their logic and then they can entertain more rational reactions. Then and only then will they be fully ready to tolerate or solve a stressful problem.

On the other hand, with a "quick fix" suggestion, they will become defensive. The reasoning goes like this: I, who know more about my problem than you, have not been able to find a solution. So who are you, who knows so little about my problem, to tell me how to solve it so quickly!? You cannot possibly help me.

Consolation, though, can produce a feeling of comfort and confidence. The comfort can compensate for the loss of control, embarrassment, or for the fear and anger over what's happened. Without the feeling of support and comfort afforded by consolation, it is difficult to do the best problem solving.

For example, if a child falls off a tricycle, it is not wise to put the child back on if he or she is still crying. It is only after comfort from consolation and a hug, and after the crying has stopped, that the child will feel reassured and confident enough to try again.

So it is with adults, but crying is disguised by complaining and defensiveness. These are clues that the pain is still impeding rational thinking and they are not ready to try again. Consolation is like a reassuring verbal hug and will help people move on. When they joke about their situation or stop sounding upset, they are ready to handle the stressful problem.

In a workshop or individual coaching session, it is possible to offer consolation about stressful problems without it turning into an uncontrolled complaining session. If complaints become an end in themselves, they can become counterproductive. Complaining also can become addictive, going nowhere, and the person's self image can become that of a hapless victim at the mercy of others. Consolation, on the other hand, goes somewhere. It raises tolerance to stay with a problem and go beyond it. The goal of consolation is tolerance and clear thinking, not discontent.

Throughout every organization and every family, people conceal complaints and their need for comfort. There is a secretive hush in hallways and quiet talk in restaurants to avoid being overheard while complaining. Complaints need to be legitimized and given the opportunity for expression through the consolation technique. That way they are processed toward more productive action.

But in some organizations or families, it is possible that the need for consolation could be misinterpreted as pampering or encouraging discontent. In that case, it might be more comfortable to select a consolation partner from outside the organization or family. No matter where we do it, we need to do it as our first line of relief. If we do not, we undercut our tolerance of the problem and make eventual discovery of solutions more difficult.

Outer Limits—It's Not Forever

Jackie calmed down about her new job with the help of Consolation. The next point I wanted to make was about the value of setting time limits. If Jackie did not demand an immediate answer or decision about her problem, she could feel less closed in, less stressed.

She needed to open her time frame by asking herself, "How long is this situation likely to go on? Will I be in this predicament one year, six months or six weeks? How long am I willing to endure it? What is my best guess?"

These are important questions. Their answers buy time, tolerable time because they help set limits and control. If Jackie decides that her situation does not have to be forever, paradoxically she would be taking an important step toward staying longer. Removing the burden of time would allow her to tap her reserves and give her best effort.

Nothing creates stress like feeling trapped or out of control. To overcome that feeling, Jackie needed to stop thinking in terms of forever. Few things are forever. She needs to start thinking of the outer limits of her problem. It is unlikely that she would become a permanent victim of her temporary problem. This too shall pass, but it is hard for Jackie to experience this truth without raising her tolerance first.

In deciding how long Jackie will allow her situation to go on, she has to pick a time period that she feels is tolerable. After that time, she can take more severe action, like confronting the boss or the supervisor of junior accounts, or bringing her resume up to date. Until that outer limit is reached, Jackie would be back in control. She and she alone would decide to stay in her job for three more days or three more months.

That decision would be empowering. She would no longer think of her situation as permanent oppression. It would become a voluntary situation in which she called the shots.

As I continued my conversation with Jackie, I said, "This is one tough spot to be in. It looks to you like your boss and that junior accounts supervisor are overlooking your deal—at least for the time being."

"Well, that's right, for the time being. It better be for the time being."

"At the outside, how long could you put up with this?"

"Hmm. I don't know, maybe a month or two."

"Why a month or two?"

"I guess it just feels right. That's about how much longer I can swallow my pride."

"OK. Sounds reasonable."

"I've been on the job, as you've pointed out, only a month and a half. I'll give them another, say, two months. I can live with that."

"How long do you think your boss would let this go on if you said nothing?"

"You got me … I suppose until his conscience troubled him. Or, until they get the junior accounts in better shape. And that shouldn't be more than, I'd say, maybe, another month."

"Well, then you're covered, I pointed out. "You said you could tolerate it for another two months. And it probably won't continue beyond about another month. This whole thing sounds troublesome but tolerable. It's been a challenge."

"That's true, but I could live nicely without it."

Even though Jackie was not totally happy about her challenge, at least thinking about the situation as a challenge, she could be less upset and more rational. She could become more open-minded, feel less ignored, suspicious or betrayed.

Silver Lining—The Good News in the Bad

Jackie's situation was far from being totally bad. There were some positives. For instance, working on the junior accounts was easy for her. The easy assignment left her with energy and time to get better oriented. There would be more time to become acquainted with the new city. And to be optimistic, from little accounts big accounts grow.

For a moment Jackie seemed reluctant to speak. Finally, I said, "I'm thinking that there's some good that could come out of this. It could be like a warm up. You know, sharpen you up. Then when you talk to the senior accounts, you'll have the answers on the tip of your tongue. That way, you'll be more credible from the beginning."

"And another thing," Jackie joined in, "I could take time to review the senior account records on the computer. Incidentally, this company's computer programs make my old company's seem like the ABC's by comparison."

"Well," I agreed, "that's the brighter side of things. Are there any other compensating advantages to this warm-up period?"

"I've had time to organize my apartment … buy some more furniture. It'll be livable a lot sooner than I expected."

The Silver Lining technique, like the other tolerance techniques, must follow Consolation. Without the catharsis of being listened to, all other techniques can be less effective or provoke defensiveness. The good news in a situation pales if the bad news is not first explored by a non-judgemental, non-advice-giving, and non-problem-fixing ally.

Jumping in too soon with the Silver Lining makes it sound like the problem is being ignored, as well as the feelings of the person.

With effective consolation given first, with its absence of lessons and lectures, the Silver Lining works well. The good news can be better accepted with the bad news.

Like all the tolerance techniques, Silver Lining can offer temporary relief until the situation can be corrected. And, in some cases where the situation is not correctable, tolerance techniques provide ongoing relief.

Reward Yourself—A Carrot on a Stick

We all need the promise of rewards. We were raised on them. They keep us running, trying a little harder, and there is comfort in anticipating their pleasures.

I wondered what rewards Jackie found meaningful. With a mild look of relief on her face, Jackie said to me, "Well, after going through that Silver Lining technique I do feel a little better about my job. But I'm going to take a break from it right now. Thanks for being my sounding board."

"You're welcome."

Looking at her watch, Jackie seemed surprised. "I have to leave soon for my workout."

"By the way, do you think of your workout as a reward for you?"

Jackie cocked her head to one side, "I don't know. Reward? I never thought about it. It's just my workout. But it's very important to me, for sure. I always feel much better after it."

"You might want to consider it as a reward."

"Why a reward?"

"Rewards are something you earn, something you look forward to. They make you feel like you've accomplished something."

"What's the big deal? What did I accomplish so far?"

"Actually, you've been patient under the circumstances. You've tried to be a team player, go along with them. Well beyond the call of duty. You deserve some reward, however small or large."

"Well, you've got something there—a reward, huh? Not a bad idea."

"For starters, your workout is a logical reward. It's easy to implement."

"That's for sure."

"What else would be something to anticipate?"

"There's a restaurant in town that I have on my list of places to go. I can go there as a reward. What else can I give myself? … How about if I buy new workout clothes? A pair of cross training shoes? If I keep this up, I won't be able to afford this job!"

"It sounds like fun."

"But I think I'll space the rewards out one a week, just in case this drags on. I've got to be realistic. It could take longer than I want."

I thought to myself how frequently we reward ourselves without thinking of it as such. And our judgment alone is the best source for determining the reward and its frequency. It reminds us that we have choices and that there are areas in our lives over which we have control.

Nothing Personal—Take the "I" Out

In stressful situations, we have a difficult time in deciding whether some of the people are truly friends or foes. For the sake of tolerating stressful problems, we need to start out with the "non-target assumption."

That is, we need to give people the benefit of the doubt and believe that we are not the deliberate target of their negative intentions. We need to at least entertain the possibility that what we see and assume does not constitute the complete situation and total reality.

In an adversarial stress state, minds close and new facts are hard to see or hear. Then stress relief and creative problem-solving are unlikely. We cannot feel relief if we think that an adversary is lurking around the corner waiting to make trouble.

What creates this adversarial state, this "under attack" attitude in stressful situations? It's the big "I." It's the self at the center of things. When we are involved with others, we are mostly aware of ourselves, our intentions, our feelings, our problems. When we encounter defensiveness, there seems to be no reason for it, or we do not have time to determine other people's intentions or the source of their defensiveness.

Usually, we see the other person's defensiveness as directed toward us, rather than their attempt to deal with their own stress, their own feelings and problems. We personalize their actions and surmise that we are the selected target of their "unjust, unkind, or unreasonable" behavior.

To help reverse this, we need to think of alternate explanations about stressful events and people. Explanations should not include "They're doing this because I am … I did … I can't … I won't … I didn't." Explanations should shift from "I" to "They." Explanations need to be based on other people's presumed good intentions or the unique problems they are confronting.

Thinking about other people's untargeted or positive intentions is an antidote to our initial negative thoughts. Our imagination, combined with our experience, can create some plausible and positive explanations about what's happening around the other person and within them.

Based on our "adversary's" problems and priorities, we can figure out alternate reasons for their behavior, reasons other than they are trying to "make our lives miserable."

Following this "Good Intentions" technique, I asked Jackie two questions, "What's going on down at your office, anyway? What would make people act like that?"

Jackie looked at me quizzically and said, "I don't get it. What do you mean?"

"I mean, what else besides getting you into senior accounts is going on? What are some of the other priorities and problems going on around them?"

Jackie got it and smiled. "Oh, yes. Of course, there are problems. Well, they're really very busy, with all those changes in departments. You know, consolidating, less duplication of effort. Then we have growth goals. We've got to reach a fifteen percent growth rate—by next year. In fact, my boss has been in meetings for weeks, with his boss. This is why he's probably been so scarce! Hmm? What else? Let me see. Oh, a big one. Hiring."

"What's that about?"

"There's a hiring freeze," Jackie answered.

"They hired you, didn't they?"

Jackie looked at me proudly but said modestly, "Well, Gary really wanted my experience. He was able to work his budget and get the OK. Besides, the interviews must have gone very well."

"With everything that's going on in the company, you're a perfect fit. It's probably easier to have you help out with the junior accounts because you're new," I explained. Their existing senior accounts people probably would resent handling junior accounts even more than you. And with your experience, you could temporarily handle those junior accounts far better than a new, inexperienced person—who they couldn't hire anyway. And it gave you a break-in period. That sounds consistent with their priority of doing more with less."

Jackie frowned. "It sounds like you're taking their side, but I can understand that position. It's a reasonable explanation. Though I wouldn't entirely rule out the possibility they've just been too busy to keep their promise to me."

"In either case, I think they deserve the benefit of the doubt. They could have good intentions."

Jackie was thoughtful. "Well … I guess … I don't know about this. What if you're wrong and they just don't care? What if I'm just a party in an underhanded plan."

"That's a fair question. But what have you lost if it's eventually true that they're going to pigeonhole you in junior accounts, that you're the target of their Machiavellian scheme?

"You've already said that you would give them two months to prove themselves. If you presume good intentions and take the "I" out of the explanations, you'll be less tense, less resentful. That way you'll keep your eyes and ears open. You'll get the most accurate picture of what's happening.

"And there's time enough to be resentful. You can always take action later on. In the meantime, make the most of it, learn, network in the company, continue your good work. And if they do prove their good intentions, you'll be glad you didn't challenge them prematurely.

They could have wound up resenting you for not trusting them."

This last thought makes Jackie ponder. "Giving them the benefit of the doubt is in my own self interest. Either way, I can't lose … that makes me feel better. I hate to lose."

Jackie seemed to be taking in my explanations as tentative possibilities. It was an important next step that could keep her mind open to discovering a bigger picture of what's going on. This could give her additional relief until the pieces of the organizational puzzle came together.

In many situations, we seldom inquire about other people's problems, intentions and priorities. We think doing that will slow us down and keep us from getting what we want. To avoid this slow down, we give ourselves fast and easy answers about why other people resist us.

This comes from our early years. We had two classifications, friend or foe. That's all our capability could handle then. Years later we still use these classifications in an effort to simplify our lives.

Friends support us and see that we get what we want. Foes resist us and impose their wills on us. If they are not with us, then they must be against us. Since they are foes, then it follows that they either don't like us or want to control us, or both.

To make "friends" in stressful situations, we have to imagine what other people are experiencing. This can be accomplished most easily through our capacity for empathy.

Empathy can begin by asking ourselves for alternative explanations. Like, what else could be going on here? What are the other people's priorities? What are their needs? What are they striving to gain? What are they striving to avoid? What explanations demonstrate that they value me?

In following this technique we do not have to become social friends with our perceived adversaries. We merely want to reduce the psychological danger we feel in the situation. To do that, we need to better understand their circumstances and motivations. When we do, they will become less threatening.

We will feel more empowered, more energized, and we will enlarge our self esteem as we shrink the problem. By stripping away the mystery surrounding the "foe," we diminish the power we have relinquished to them.

We can learn something from a child's fear of a shadowy figure in a closet, or a silent intruder under a bed. These are also presumed foes. This is also the child's admission of vulnerability. With limited power and reasoning, the child needs proof that there is no foe. Turning on the lights and having a powerful parent look in the closet or under the bed is reassuring.

Adults, however, have the reasoning and power to provide their own reassurances. We can "turn on the lights ourselves, check the closets and look under the bed." By depersonalizing our explanations and looking for alternate explanations of good intentions, we can help ourselves do that. It can help us cast out the shadows and sleep more soundly with the comforting knowledge that we are not the target of intruders who have bad intentions.

Comic Relief—Timeout from Trouble

Staying serious about our troubles adds to the stress. We need to have a change of pace with some laughter. In case laughter is misconstrued as frivolous, we need to remind ourselves that laughter is a serious matter.

Laugh and the whole world laughs with you, and you feel better. Cry and you cry alone, and you feel better. No doubt you have heard the expression "There is a fine line between laughter and tears." Both can be cleansing and both can be exhausting. Both engage all the organ systems of our body.

Watch children and see how instantaneously they switch from laughter to tears and back again. Watch how a baby's whole body participates in laughter or tears, the head bobbing and the arms flailing and the legs kicking. Adults have many of the same reactions, too. With a big laugh we throw our head back and come forward with an expulsion of sound, and air is pushed out of our lungs as the diaphragm contracts and releases. If it is a small laugh the process is scaled down, but it is all there.

When we laugh, more oxygen is taken into the lungs and is carried to our brain by the bloodstream. This makes us feel refreshed, alert. Muscles in our neck, shoulders and torso are stretched to break up the fatigue producing lactic acid deposits that accumulated there from the day's stress. This also refreshes us. Less apparent, chemicals in the brain are released to fight pain and boost the body's immune system.

These physiological benefits of laughing—or laughing until we cry, or crying until we laugh—are comparable to jogging. In this case, all the action is in the inside.

But beyond these physical advantages of laughter, there are important psychological ones. For one thing, laughter breaks the mind-clouding intensity and seriousness of many situations. It provides an emotional distance from problems, a distance that adds the possibility of a more objective look at a situation or a problem.

In a work setting, tears and laughter are taboo. Somehow if we maintain a furrowed brow and tightened lips, our work product should improve. Work is serious business and business is serious work, but there is no need to take them so seriously. Without disrespect for work or business, it is important to gain perspective and distance.

Yes, if the climate was continuously frivolous and concentration lapsed from people standing around telling jokes all day, we would have a serious problem. But the humor break is just that—a break, a break in the stress and a time to be refreshed physically and psychologically.

For laughter to have a therapeutic effect, it should not be hostile or demeaning to the laugher or the laughed at. Someone need not be the butt of a joke or the object of ridicule. Laughter is restorative when it stems from comments on the human condition or our momentary misery. Laughter delights when we are surprised. And laughter nurtures us when we confront our common foibles with a kind touch and accept our embarrassments with patience and love.

Take the situation with Jackie and her new job, for instance. What's so funny about the boss not keeping his promise, and that junior accounts supervisor keeping Jackie for the supervisor's own department?

I said to Jackie, "Let's see, I've given you a number of techniques to increase your tolerance to your situation—and to your boss. And, yes, to that junior accounts supervisor."

Jackie nodded her head and said, "To be perfectly frank with you, well, let's see. How can I put this? Some of your techniques make more sense to me than others. There. I said it. I hope I haven't hurt your feelings, have I?"

"Whatever works for you is fine with me. That's why you have choices. They all can't be meaningful to you—but I can hope!"

Jackie grinned. "I do like that reward approach. That's painless. Though I could go broke, if I'm stressed too long."

"You said you would set a time limit of two months. Are you sure you wouldn't like to extend it to four? Think of all the additional rewards in that extra time."

"No, please. No extra time," Jackie pleaded. "Those rewards I selected—there's only so much I can buy. And I don't like to eat out that much, either."

I kidded Jackie, "I didn't say anything before, but your rewards are transferable. I'll gladly go to a fine restaurant in your place."

"No, thanks," Jackie fired back. "I have a better idea. I'll transfer those rewards to my boss and the junior accounts supervisor."

"I'm wondering something," Jackie. On an outside chance that your boss doesn't come around in your time limit, what would it be like? What would you do? What would he do?"

Jackie pondered the questions. "I'd probably tell them I'm leaving, and that supervisor of junior accounts would plead with me not to go—on her knees."

"That's a great fantasy," I agreed. "I can see her clutching at your ankles, trying to hold you back as you move toward the door, dragging her with you."

"Yeah, and my boss is blocking the door. He won't let us through. He shows me a picture of his wife and kids. But I'm still determined to go. He spreads his arms across the door and reminds me about his growth targets—and what his boss will do to him if he doesn't make it."

I add quickly, "Then he makes you another big promise. He'll handle the junior accounts himself!"

Jackie's smile broadened. "Now my boss is making sense to me. But I won't agree to stay unless the junior accounts supervisor reports to me!"

I played along. "It sounds like a plan."

"This is more like it." Jackie's pleasure was apparent. "This job is turning out great. I'm a legend in my own mind!"

We laughed and decided to meet tomorrow. I wrote the appointment in my calendar.

We did not take her problem lightly. On the contrary, our laughter was comic relief over a serious matter. We were laughing seriously.

Which Tolerance Techniques Will Work Best for You?

Consolation—Misery Needs Company

Outer Limits—It's Not Forever

Silver Lining—The Good News in the Bad

Good Intentions—It Was Nothing Personal

Reward Yourself—Put a Carrot on a Stick

Comic Relief—Time Out from Trouble

Tolerance techniques provide ongoing relief. The purpose is to clear the head and calm the body to better live with stress and the problems creating it.

Try Out Section

Consider the list of tolerance techniques below. They can help you better tolerate stressful problems and stressful people. Remember, you may feel more comfortable with some techniques than others. Try as many as you can.

Try Consolation—Misery Loves Company

Describe your problem. Write it down or say it to yourself.

____

____

____

Remember, the key to consolation is communicating a sympathetic understanding. A supportive and loyal ally is needed—one who listens but offers no advice, makes no judgments and is an ally who does not give a lecture or a lesson.

The objective of consolation is to become less emotional and discharge negative thoughts, to feel the situation is understood and make room for more positive thoughts.

If you have someone on whom you rely, tell them you do not want to fix the problems yet, but need someone to hear you out.

That person is ________________________________

There are a number of expressions that you can have the other person say to you, or you can say to yourself.

Consolation—Opening Statements:

I'm sorry this is happening.
Anyone would have trouble with this situation.
I'm on your side. This is tough.
You must have lots of patience.
That's a lot to deal with here.
When it rains, it pours.
You can count on me.

Which of these opening statements—or something else you might prefer—would be most meaningful to you?

____

____

____

Beyond the opening statement, what response would you want from this person?

___

___

___

Have an imaginary conversation about the problem.

Other person

___

___

___

Me

___

___

___

Other person

___

___

___

Me

___

___

___

Try Outer Limits—It's Not Forever

When we are deeply immersed in a problem situation, we often lose time perspective. It feels as if this is going to be forever. It will not, but we have to be reminded. By setting a time limit, it allows us to feel in control. It is reassuring to think that we will not be permanent victims of this temporary problem.

What is the situation?

____

____

____

To set the outer limits, write down or ask your self the following questions:

How long is this event likely to last?

____

____

____

On what do I base my estimate?

____

____

____

How long am I prepared to endure it?

____

____

____

On what do I base my endurance estimate?

____

____

____

Is it realistic? If not, what is?

____

____

____

Making a commitment to set aside a problem for a specific time makes you feel in control and frees energy which is no longer spent on stress.

Try Silver Lining—Good News in the Bad

Even in the most difficult situation, there is usually a benefit—some good news. In situations where there is a severe loss or tragedy, however, there is not likely to be a benefit. Or if there is, we may not be ready to look at it. Though even in death it is common to hear people say, “He’s in a better place, now”; “At least her suffering is over.” It helps the stressful grief.

But the majority of everyday stressful events can become more tolerable when we can think of some compensating personal payoff.

Describe a stressful event or a stressful person. Write it down or say it out loud.

____

____

____

Ask yourself the question, "What are the benefits in the event or with the person?"

____

____

____

Stay with it! You can think of at least one, maybe more.

____

____

____

Try Reward Yourself—A Carrot on a Stick

What are some of your customary rewards: an ice cream cone, new clothes, a swim, sex, a movie, a new music CD, a run in the park? The reward list is common to all of us, but we require different frequencies and different quantities. A "carrot on the stick" technique dangles the promise of compensating pleasure, if we can just endure a little discomfort, or pain, for a little more time.

When we consciously set out to reward ourselves, we are invoking our sense of control. This counterbalances the feeling of being out of control in stressful situations. It is important, therefore, to make the reward a conscious choice. We must be aware that the pleasure is compensation for the pain. If the pleasure is randomly experienced and does not connect to the stressful situation, it will not feel empowering. It will feel like generalized, momentary well-being that dissipates all too quickly and is unconnected to an event or person.

We need rewards outside of the problem situation, something special.

What are your favorite rewards?

- Reading a book
- Eating ice cream
- Swimming
- Buying clothes
- Running a few miles
- Having sex
- Walking in the park
- Listening to music
- Taking time for sports
- Seeing a movie
- Going to a restaurant

Dangle a carrot from a stick and you'll have some compensating pleasure. Choose a reward and consciously connect it to the event you are trying to tolerate. Pleasure randomly experienced will not be as effective as receiving the reward specifically for your willingness to put up with the problem.

My rewards are

____

____

____

Try Nothing Personal—Take the "I" Out

In a stressful situation, it is difficult to determine whether people are friends or foes. What makes it more difficult is that we guess at people's intentions. Often, we assume bad intentions, and that we are the deliberate target of their behavior. This way we feel more ready and protected for possible trouble. In this ready state, fear, anxiety and anger can be aroused. Clear thinking is more difficult and new facts are hard to see and hear.

Because our big "I," our self, is the center of things, we think that we are the target and we see stressful people's defensiveness as an attack on us, rather than their possible attempt to deal with their own problems and stress.

Our "I" must be temporarily removed. We cannot say, "They did this because "I" (did, am, can't, won't)." The other person's reactions or behavior must be seen as unique to them and their motivations, not connected in any way to us.

To get outside of ourselves, see a bigger picture and develop more tolerance, here are questions we need to ask about the other people in the situation.

What is the problem in the current situation?

____

____

____

What problems do they have that could be creating stress and causing defensiveness?

____

____

____

Do they have other priorities besides making life "miserable" for us?

____

____

____

What would be their explanation—that does not include us—for what's happening?

____

____

____

There seems little reason or time to find out the source of other people's stress and defensiveness. But the only way we can get relief is to give people the benefit of the doubt. We need to assume good intentions and get into their shoes, surmise what's happening from *their* perspective. This clears our head and calms us down and helps when we try to solve our problems in the situation.

Try Comic Relief—Time Out from Trouble

Laughing is serious business. In stressful situations, laughter is an important change of pace and it creates an emotional distance from problems. As a result of a hearty laugh, the muscles in our upper torso relax, more oxygen enters the lungs, healing chemicals in the brain release, and generally we feel refreshed.

To lighten a heavy problem, recall a recent funny situation or the last time you had a hearty laugh. See the situation in your mind's eye and see yourself laughing and having a good time.

Describe it

____

____

____

Consciously smile. With a smile on your face, tell yourself or someone else about what happened that made you laugh.

If laughter doesn't come, prime it with a simulated laugh.

If you can't think of a funny situation, have some people tell you their favorite jokes.

When you have more time, see a funny movie or TV show.

Keep a smile on your face. It's hard to be down when your face is up.

Have someone tickle you.

Take time out from trouble and laugh, laugh, laugh.

CHAPTER 7

GIVE PROBLEMS THE THIRD DEGREE

Probing Questions that Produce Solutions

The next step is to consider permanent solutions to stressful problems. These solutions are aimed at stopping stress at its source. To that end, we have to give stressful problems the third degree. They need the hot, white light of analysis and probing questions. There are four solutions techniques with probing questions that help us solve problems and stop stress at its source.

Solutions Techniques

Test Probabilities of Worst and Best Outcomes
Replace Ill-logics With Logical Thinking
Reduce Old Reactions for Emotional Control
Find Overlooked Alternatives to Solve Problems

Under stress, one problem is to gain control of emotions that flood our thinking. Often our emotional thinking is that the worst will happen. By testing the probability of the worst happening, it is possible to think more objectively and realistically.

Testing probabilities quiets our emotions. When we see the inevitable difference between our emotional expectations of worst outcomes and the more rational probabilities in the situation, we can be assured and even amused.

For example, in my next session with Jackie, the day after our first session on tolerance techniques, I wanted to prepare her for some effective problem solving. Remember Jackie and her new job, the boss and the junior accounts supervisor. Jackie was hired to handle senior accounts, but she had been working on junior accounts for a period way beyond what was necessary for an orientation to the company and the senior accounts job for which he had been hired.

Jackie had been frustrated and suspicious about her boss's intentions. It appeared that the promise of working on senior accounts was just a lure to get Jackie to come to work for him. However, one of the ways Jackie had raised her tolerance about working on junior accounts was by setting a time limit of two more months. She would wait and see if her boss's organizational pressures changed and if he kept his promise of placing Jackie on senior accounts.

In the company conference room, Jackie and I continued our dialogue over steaming cups of coffee. Our mood was thoughtful and relaxed.

"Well, Jackie, have you given any more thought to your problem?"

"Yes, but I'm taking no chances. I think the worst. That way I won't feel so bad if I don't like what happens."

"Would you like to look at what might happen," I offered. "We can test the probabilities about the outcome of the situation?"

Pouring another cup of coffee, Jackie said emphatically, "Let's do it."

Testing Probabilities

"OK. Think of the three worst possible outcomes to your situation. Think of the most negative things that could happen." I fished in my briefcase for a notepad. "Here, I'll list them on the pad."

"This will be easy," Jackie assured me. "I've thought about it enough. Worst outcomes. No. 1: I'm typecast as a junior accounts person for the rest of my career. No. 2: I have to quit and relocate again. No. 3: Hmm. Let's see. I can't think of another one."

"Keep thinking."

Jackie got it. "No. 3: I'll get so stale on those junior accounts that I'll lose my ambition. My motivation will be shot."

"All right, now list the best outcomes from the situation."

"This is going to take a little longer. I haven't given this too much thought."

"That's usually what happens."

A flash of recognition came over Jackie's face. "I've got it! No. 1 best outcome … they're so appreciative of my helping out on those junior accounts that they give me some really select senior accounts as a reward."

I nodded. "That's a good one. I hope that comes true for you."

"Well, let's see now, what's my No. 2? Try this. No. 2 … my boss sees how good I am at junior accounts and makes me supervisor of that department—and puts the current supervisor of junior accounts covering senior accounts in my old place!"

"You've got the idea. One more best outcome."

"No. 3. … No. 3? How's this? Next month the boss thanks me and puts me on the senior accounts and I become one of his top performers."

I placed the pad in front of Jackie. "Here are your three worst and three best outcomes I've written on the pad."

Worst Outcomes:

1. Junior accounts forever
2. Quit and relocate
3. Lose motivation

Best Outcomes:

1. Get the top senior accounts
2. Become supervisor of junior accounts
3. On senior accounts, become a top performer

"Now what are your predictions? Give me your estimates, in percentages. What are the chances that these things will happen to you? Take the pen and write the percentages next to the outcomes."

Jackie took the pen and became thoughtful. As she wrote down the probabilities, she smiled, shaking her head in disbelief. She sighed. "Here it is. I'm surprised."

"Surprised?"

"Yes, surprised. I can't believe how real those worst outcomes were to me. But probabilities? Look at those percentages. It's so different after I think about it."

She handed me the pad.

Worst Outcomes, Percentages:

1. Junior accounts forever, 5%
2. Quit and relocate, 30%
3. Lose motivation, 10%

Best Outcomes, Percentages:

1. Get top senior accounts, 20%
2. Become supervisor of junior accounts, 1%
3. On senior accounts, become a top performer, 85%

Jackie was still surprised. "Before I thought about this carefully, all three worst outcomes felt 95% real! They really did."

"The gloom and doom always seems worse when you're in the middle of a problem. Until you give the problem the third degree, subject it to a more rational, unemotional mood, a logical structure, it's hard to think of solutions, or make a realistic evaluation."

"I think I get it," Jackie said with the pleasure of discovery. "When something is very important to you and gets threatened, it's like a knee-jerk reaction. Career is my top priority, and it looked like it was put on hold, out of my control. I felt that I was losing momentum, slowed down by my boss—or the self-interest of the supervisor. No wonder I felt so much stress. But I guess the more stress I felt, the less logical I became. Wow."

"It's that simple and that difficult at the same time."

"I'll tell you one thing." Jackie said with conviction, "Now I'm in a much better frame of mind to solve the problem."

Replace Ill-logics

"Jackie, you still have one more step before you try to find workable solutions. You have to replace your 'ill-logics' with clear thinking."

"Replace my what?" Jackie questioned with an edgy tone. She thought she had it all wrapped up.

"Ill-logics," I repeated. "It's the kind of logic that locks you into the problem so you can't solve it. Eventually, the frustration and stress wear you down, makes you … you know … ill…ill-logics."

Jackie looked solemn. "Sounds awful. I'm half kidding and half serious."

"But that's the thing. Ill-logics keep us stuck. They block us from fresh thinking that would help us solve problems, eliminate the source of stress.

"Give me an example."

"Here, let me write down the five ill-logics for you."

Inflated Logic (Exaggeration)
Polar Logic (Either/or thinking)
Contagious Logic (Generalizing)
Leaping Logic (Jumping to conclusions)
Fantasy Logic (Unrealistic expectations)

Jackie nodded her head up and down, signifying that she recognized some of them. "I can tell you which of these keeps me stuck. I can see where I made a lot of trouble for myself." She wrote something on the pad.

I stretched to see what she had written. "Not to be nosey, but what did you write?"

"I put down two that I might be using in this situation. Inflated Logic and Leaping Logic. You better run through these to make sure I understand them."

"All five of them?"

"All five of them."

Inflated Logic—Exaggeration

"Well, then, briefly, there is Inflated Logic. It's a form of exaggeration. Emotions inflate our picture of the problem way out of proportion. The blown-up version becomes real in our mind. For instances, on your Worst Outcomes list, you had thought about outcomes that overwhelmed you. But when you put down the actual probabilities, you could see how much you had inflated them."

"That I did."

"Inflating the size of a problem has another purpose. It gets more attention. There is the woe-is-me factor, getting some support and sympathy about the problem. Small problems can get overlooked and do not elicit any concern from other people. Large problems can make us feel more significant, more important.

Polar Logic—Either/or Thinking

"Polar Logic, that's the next one. I wrote it down. It's the all-or-nothing logic, thinking in terms of either/or, right or wrong, good or bad, strong or weak, happy or sad. I could give you more examples."

Jackie raised her hand in a "stop" gesture. "I've got it. The 'or' locks us into thinking we're one thing and nothing else. If we're bad, we're bad and that's it.

"When we use polar logic, a problem situation is seen as black or white with no shades of gray. We think at the extremes, no middle ground."

Jackie looked a little relieved. "Polar logic is not a problem for me, but I know some people at work who use it. They're not easy to deal with in that frame of mind."

"I can suggest a good habit for them to get into. Substitute 'and' for 'or'."

"Jackie responded, "Like good and bad, strong and weak. There's a little bit of both in everything, and everybody."

"That's right," I agreed. "But it's easy for someone to forget and slip into Polar Logic. A case in point is performance reviews. If a person's boss gives many positive comments but mentions one or two areas for improvement, the person may go away feeling negative. With Polar Logic they think if it isn't all positive, then it must be negative. Either you like my work or you don't."

"I'm glad that's not one of my ill-logics, Jackie said. I have enough trouble with Inflated Logic." She looked at the pad and asked, "What's this Contagious Logic? Does that mean you can catch it? Just kidding!"

Contagious Logic—Generalizing

"No, not as bad as that, but it does mean that Contagious Logic can spread from one situation to another. Or it can spread from how we think about one person to how we think about many people. We go from making a judgment that is valid in one particular situation, or about one person, and let it spread to other people or situations that are not really similar. We accept our appraisal of the situation or the person as truth without questioning the true likeness of the new to the old situation."

Thoughtfully, Jackie considered the explanation. "I think I understand, though I'm not totally sure. Let me say it another way. You form some kind of judgment about a situation, or person in a situation. Then you get into another situation that's truly different, but you still act like it's the old situation. You see it with old eyes and don't see how the new situation or the new person is different."

"You've got it," I confirmed.

Extending my explanation, Jackie said, "My supervisor's like that. She had a couple of the junior accounts people mess up a project. It undercut her work so much that she began not trusting any of us to handle the same kind of project. Before you knew it, she was the only one doing those projects."

"That's a typical reaction."

"They're excellent workers. There are some talented people in that group."

"Your supervisor is losing out on some good resources. I'll bet that she'll try to figure out how to cut her workload but overlook that her Contagious Logic is an important part of the problem."

"I'll think about that."

"Well, let me give you something else to think about. Think about Leaping Logic."

"Oh, no. Do we have to?' Jackie joked. That's one of my ill-logics."

"You can take it."

Leaping Logic—Jumping to Conclusions

"Leaping Logic is taking a few facts and drawing far-reaching but incorrect conclusions. That's because a few facts is all we need to trigger a conclusion. Then we act as if the conclusion is based on complete facts and careful analysis. We rush to be an expert with the right answer."

"Oh, that hits home. I've jumped to a few conclusions in my time. It's hard to shake me loose when I do."

"Leaping Logic can be high-speed thinking. We have so much momentum we can't stop to get the facts. We go full throttle down the highway until we crash—like make a major mistake, or have a run-in with somebody—then we realize there was more to the situation than we took time to find out."

"Tell me about it. Sometimes I feel embarrassed."

"When we're feeling stressed, this ill-logic can sneak in. Sometimes we don't hear or see what's going on. We want to relieve our stress quickly. We don't feel we can afford the time to get more facts. We want certainty—fast. And that gives us the illusion of control. That's much better than feeling out of control, which is one of the reasons for our stress in the first place."

"Well, I've certainly felt out of control in this job."

"I'll bet you have. You said that you felt blocked from reaching your career goals. When we can't influence someone, or something that's important to us, we're bound to feel powerless."

"I sure want quick answers." Jackie realized. "I want to know where I stand with the senior accounts. So I jump to a few conclusions from very few facts. That does give me the feeling I know what's going on even though I might be all wrong."

"Your Leaping Logic gives you quick answers, but the quick answers compound the problem. They create a false reality."

"I sound like the dog chasing its tail—going in circles, lots of action but going nowhere."

"Exactly, that's the stress cycle."

"Well, I'd like to break the cycle."

"You can. You already have."

Jackie agreed.

"You tested the possible outcomes in your situation and their probabilities. And you have insight into your own ill-logics, Inflated Logic and Leaping Logic. They can keep you stuck in a problem."

"I don't like loose ends. I like to complete things I set out to do," Jackie said. "What's next here on your ill-logics list?" Jackie scanned the pad. "Here. The last one on the list is Fantasy Logic. Now that intrigues me."

Fantasy Logic—Unrealistic Expectations

"Take a guess," I challenged. "Fantasy Logic?"

"Maybe it's like daydreaming. It's so outlandish that it will never happen?"

"Not bad. It's like wishful thinking," I added. "We expect the impossible—from ourselves, other people, or the situation. It won't happen, but we go on acting as if our expectations are obtainable. Then we get mad at ourselves or other people when they're not meeting our expectations. Our wishes are powerful and we go on expecting to overcome the offending reality. But it's just not possible."

"That sounds self-defeating."

I nodded my head in agreement. "It can be frustrating, and make us angry. But we hold on tightly to the unrealistic expectations."

"We're taught not to be quitters," Jackie reminded me.

"I know. But the wish can be more compelling than reality. Things aren't going to be what we want them to be unless we turn the wish into work—if it is truly workable!"

Jackie said, "You can say that about any of the ill-logics. They'll keep you running in circles, making you dizzy, so you can't move ahead. When you break the circle with clear thinking, you're on your way."

Jackie cocked her head to one side. A broad grin telegraphed her pleasure. "Hey, guess what? When you give up the ill-logics, you know what you have? … Well-logics! Clear thinking helps keep you well. Well-logics!"

I smiled. "Really, that's a powerful way of putting it,"

"OK, what's next?" Jackie asked. She was eager to move on.

Reducing Old Reactions

"To summarize, you've tested probabilities as well as the worst and best outcomes in your situation to see it more realistically. Then you've replaced ill-logics with clear thinking to do better problem solving. Next is reducing old reactions that inflame your present situation and add more stress."

I continued, "It's natural to focus attention on what's easily observed. But stressful problems can remind us of old reactions from past situations. We ignore and seldom verbalize them. These old reactions go unnoticed, yet they inflame our stress, making it linger even when we take care of the present problem."

I turned over the note pad and listed the old reactions that can compound our stress. Jackie watched intently as I listed them.

Old Reactions

Deadlines Imposed by Ourselves or Others

Vague Information or Objectives

Unclear or Excessive Authority

Nonsupport from Key People

Overload from Too Much Work or Too Little Experience

Failing on a Project or a Major Mistake

Invasion of Territory

Criticism of Competency or Integrity

Resistance and Opposition

Looking up from the note pad I asked Jackie, "In your current situation, which of these old reactions adds to your stress?"

"Let me see. I don't know. Oh, there." Jackie points to Resistance and Opposition. "I don't like people standing in my way. Nonsupport is another. That's a close second. If I think people are not backing me up, I get upset."

"What about in your last job?"

"The same way. But I got resistance on different things. It was having my ideas turned down. That stressed me!"

"What's being blocked here?"

"Here? Just my career! Wow, just thinking about it gets me stressed."

"Is this a recent thing, this reaction to 'resistance,' or has that been going on a long time?"

"Hmm. You know, I guess that goes far back. I always wanted what I wanted when I wanted it. And I want those senior accounts—now!"

"I'll take a guess. Your strong reaction to 'Resistance and Opposition' runs through many stressful situations in your life. Getting the senior accounts is one of several situations that triggered it."

"You nailed that one. I want my boyfriend to marry me this year—as soon as possible. But he doesn't want to leave his job—or move here—not until things are more settled for me. That pushes my buttons."

"He has some good reasons not to get married yet, but you seem to focus primarily on the resistance you experience."

"I do, I do!"

I thought a moment. "By just being aware that your old reaction is inflaming your current situation, you can reduce its effects. And it will help in other situations, like getting over the resistance from you getting what you want on this job. Your awareness will help you have more control over how you respond to 'resistance' in general."

Absorbed, Jackie looked far away. She seemed to be remembering something. "I'm just thinking. I've been this way a long time."

"How long?"

"Good question. Well, it actually goes back to my Dad and me. When people got in his way, he was a good guy about it. He just let things happen to him. If he didn't get what he wanted, it was OK. He never pushed for it."

"What's wrong with that?"

"My dad didn't seem to have much fight in him. He gave up too easy. I thought I did, too. I remember my brother and I talking about it. We made a vow. Nobody was going to push us around like that. I'm getting emotional just thinking about it."

I jumped in. "That vow—not being too easy—or to put it another way, that fear of being too easy, follows you around wherever you go. Realistically now, if you don't get what you want in one situation, it doesn't prove you're too easy. It proves you couldn't get what you wanted in that situation. You know, there's enough going on in the present without overloading it with the past."

"That's easy for you to say," Jackie replied.

"Well, maybe it's time for you to make another vow—a vow that has the advantage of your more mature experience."

"OK. What's the vow?"

"To keep trying to get what you want, but with less of the old reaction about resistance. You can say to yourself, 'I'm in control. I'm not powerless. I have options. Nobody but myself will judge me as too easy.'"

"That's not bad. I do judge. I'm tough on myself. And I probably do have more options than I take time to think about. I really don't have to force the issue."

"You've got it. As the martial arts have instructed, you don't have to meet force head on with greater force to overcome the resistance. The irony is that the easier you are, the stronger you'll be to find solutions and get what you want."

"Point well taken."

Find Overlooked Alternatives

"Now let's work on the problem, Jackie. Start with a clear statement of the problem."

"That's easy. I have to get my boss to say, 'Now is the time to put Jackie into senior accounts.'"

"Fine. What about the supervisor of junior accounts?"

"Well, I have to overcome any reluctance she might have to letting me go."

"So let's look at three alternatives to solve the problem of the boss's slowness to act. We also need to look at the supervisor's possible investment in your staying put."

Jackie protested, "Three alternatives? How about settling for two?"

"Perhaps. But let's try for three. The more options you have the more you feel in control."

Reaching for the note pad, Jackie said, "I'll try to write the alternatives down."

Before Jackie could pick up the note pad, I reached for it and said, "Let me divide the page into three vertical columns. At the top of the page, I'll label the columns Solution 1, 2 and 3. Then I'll list four questions down the side of the page extending across the columns, dividing the page into four equal horizontal sections."

Jackie studied the page and said, "You've done this before, haven't you?"

"Yes, it works well," I answered.

Sighing and taking a deep breath, Jackie requested more time to think about her answers. "I can do this later."

"Once you get into it, it goes fast."

Fifteen minutes passed. Jackie was involved. As she finished the last question, she shook her head and smiled. "I didn't think I had any options, but here I am with three. I don't know which is best. But here they are for better or worse."

Reading across the top of the page, I reviewed Jackie's three alternate solutions. Then I read down to see how she answered the other questions about each alternative.

FIND OVERLOOKED ALTERNATIVES

What are three alternative ways of solving the problem?		
Alternative 1	**Alternative 2**	**Alternative 3**
Make friends with the sr. accts. people. Find out where sr. accts. has problems and show how I can help.	Ask the boss how much more time he plans to keep me on jr. accts. Remind him of his promise.	Help jr. accts' supervisor trust her people more, so she won't need my sr. know-how.
What are the advantages of each alternative?		
Become more knowledgeable about sr. accts. and demonstrate my worth to boss and to the organization.	Gets to the decision maker and reminds him of my value on senior accounts. Quickly know results.	Removes block to my progress. Helps supervisor to rely on her own jr. accts. people.
What are the disadvantages of each alternative?		
Sr. accts people aren't too keen about working with jr. accts. people. Not sure I can get support.	Boss could feel I'm pressuring him and I don't trust him to keep promise. I'm impatient.	Not my place to help her. Extra work for me. It's hard to change people.
How can you overcome these disadvantages?		
Find at least one jr. accts. person who would help and support my cause. Become friends.	Practice asking boss tactfully. Show him I'm not pressuring, just checking, eager to show what I can do for the org.	Include another jr. accts. person whom supervisor could trust. Tell sup'r my sr. accts. know-how can prevent mistakes.

I reviewed Jackie's answers. We had something to work with here. "Let's explore your solutions so you can decide which one to try."

"I'm game," Jackie said enthusiastically. "Explore away."

"First of all," I said, "you've done some creative thinking."

"Until I put my mind to it, I didn't think I had much to say about it. It surprised me. I guess I have some options, after all. Just might work."

As I read over Jackie's alternatives again, I was impressed with the possibilities. "Well, which one is it going to be? Confront the boss, work through the senior accounts people, or help the supervisor let you go?"

"I see these approaches as having different risks and rewards," Jackie said thoughtfully, "and going right to the boss saves time, but if I make a mistake the damage is done. On the other hand, if I work with senior accounts people, there's less risk but they don't have much influence. That leaves the supervisor. This is where I'm supposed to be, with her. This is where they want me for now, so this is where I can prove myself. And I can help the supervisor feel secure enough to let me move up."

"What if that approach doesn't work? What will you do instead?"

"Then I like the idea of going directly to the boss—tactfully. If that doesn't get me what I want, it's off to the senior accounts people. Then, of course, there's the last resort. The big 'Q.' Quit. But I'm confident that won't be necessary. I've got two other options that seem good to me. From zero options to three. Let me tell you, it felt rotten thinking I had no options. I feel back in charge of what's happening."

"That's empowerment. You took charge of the situation by discovering your overlooked alternatives. You became bigger than the problem facing you, and you reduced the problem down to a manageable size."

"No wonder I feel better."

On that note, Jackie suggested we go to lunch, recommending this restaurant she wanted to try. We went off to lunch feeling very good. During our lunch, our conversation soon turned to sports and politics. We welcomed the timeout from stress and problem solving.

TRY OUT SECTION

Try Testing Probabilities

As your focus, use the same stressful event that you used for trying the tolerance techniques, or choose a new stressful problem. The more techniques you try, the more powerful will be your skills in problem solving.

Under stress we expect the worst. Psychologists call this "catastrophic expectations." We need to put our negative thinking to a reality test, asking ourselves the question: "How likely are the worst case consequences?" Can the situation be that bad? Yes, sometimes it is, but we have to find out which time this is.

To do this, first, restate the stressful event and problem.

____

____

____

List the three worst outcomes.

1. ______________________________

____

____

2. ______________________________

____

____

3. ______________________________

____

____

Next, list the three best outcomes.

1. ______________________________

____

____

2. ______________________________

____

____

3. ______________________________

____

____

Estimate the probability of each of the above actually happening (0% = no chance, 100% = certain to happen).

Describe what you now think is the likely outcome of the event.

____

____

____

How do you feel about the results of the probability test?

____

____

____

Try Replacing Ill-logics

Faulty thinking patterns—illogics—stop us from solving problems. These perpetuate stress. Replacing illogics with healthy logic can help us. From the descriptions below, select or check (✓) one or several illogics that divert you from clear thinking. Then apply the well-logics that provide the remedy.

Inflated Logic—Exaggeration ( )

We overstate what is going on and magnify the problem until what is happening is blown out of proportion.

Counteracted by

Minimizing and understating the problem and the situation to bring them down to size. Apply a corrective percentage to your perception of the event, like a magnification factor of 10, 20, or 30 percent? Check it out with other people. See if they think it is as serious as you do.

My problem as I see it:

____

____

____

As others see it:

____

____

____

Polar Logic—Either/or Thinking ( )

With no possible middle ground, we see problems as black or white, right or wrong, win or lose, for me or against me. Our thinking is at the extremes.

Counteracted by

Expanding the middle options, looking for shades of gray, finding compromise positions for win/win solutions. Use the word "and" in your reasoning rather than "or."

My polar problem:

____

____

____

Middle-ground solutions:

____

____

____

Contagious Logic—Generalizing ( )

From one event, we carry over judgments to many other situations or people. This prevents us from seeing what's different or unique about new situations and new people.

Counteracted by

Isolating what's different in this situation even though it may appear to be similar. List similarities and differences.

Is my current problem or situation like one I've had before?

If yes, how is it alike?

____

____

____

How is it different?

____

____

____

Leaping Logic—Jumping To Conclusions ( )

Without sufficient information, we quickly arrive at invalid conclusions feeling assured that we have the total picture.

Counteracted by

Suspending judgment and looking for more information. Say to yourself, "The jury's not in on this one yet. What else am I not seeing here? What else would motivate someone to do such a thing?

What is my judgment on my problem or situation?

____

____

____

What other information might be available?

____

____

____

How else can I defer my judgment?

____

____

____

Fantasy Logic—Unrealistic Expectations

Expecting things that are beyond ourselves and other people, we ignore all realistic evidence that our demands are impossible to accomplish. This leads to frustration, disappointment and anger toward all involved in the situation.

Counteracted by

Rating your expectations on a 10 point scale from realistic, 10, to unrealistic, 1. Check it out with others in similar situations and compare their rating of how realistic your expectations or demands are.

My situation:

___

___

___

My expectations:

___

___

___

What part or parts of my expectations are unrealistic?

___

___

___

How can I modify or let go my expectations?

___

___

___

Try Reducing Old Reactions

In your current stressful event, which of the old reactions listed below still pop up and create additional stress for you?

Old Reactions

- Deadlines Imposed by Others
- Vague Information or Objectives
- Unclear or Excessive Authority

- Nonsupport by People
- Failing by Losing Out or Messing Up
- Invasion of Our Territory
- Criticism of Competence or Integrity
- Resistance or Opposition
- Deprivation of What We Need and Want
- Overload from Too Much Work or Too Little Experience

Now from the above list titled Old Reactions, select one to use for the following questionnaire.

Here are some questions that can help you think more clearly and objectively about the old reactions, the past in your present.

Questions to Reduce Reactions

Answer as many as you can.

1. When did I first experience this or these reactions?

___

___

___

2. What decisions did I make as a result of this experience?

___

___

___

3. How do those decisions influence my current reactions?

____

____

____

4. What positive consequences resulted from those decisions?

____

____

____

5. What negative consequences resulted from those decisions?

____

____

____

6. How is the present situation different from the past?

____

____

____

7. What do I know now that I didn't know then?

____

____

____

Whenever you encounter stress from a problem with an event or a person, check to see if one of your old reactions is aroused. After you have identified the reactions, respond to the seven questions. In a short while you may need only to ask yourself questions 6 and 7. Eventually, only the answer to question 7 may be necessary to release your old reactions and to clear the past from the present.

Try Finding Overlooked Alternatives

If we have tried unsuccessfully to solve a stressful problem, we often feel frustrated and that there is no way out. The intensity of our stress narrows what we see and hear. Though we think that we have left no stone unturned, it is most likely that several new alternatives have been overlooked.

My situation:

____

____

____

First, brainstorm alternative solutions to your stressful problem. To realize as many new solutions as possible, it is important to follow the key rules of brainstorming:

- Suspend judgment and early evaluation.
- The goal is not how good but how many solutions.
- Avoid statements that stop the flow of ideas such as "it will never work," "it can't be done," "they'll never let it happen."
- Build one idea on top of another.
- Generate as many solutions as possible.
- Be open to possibilities.
- Do not get into ideas about implementing the solutions.

To spark your effort, a brainstorming partner can be invaluable, or brainstorm yourself following the rules above.

When you finish brainstorming, select three alternatives for further analysis before deciding on one.

My three alternatives:

a. ______________________________

____

b. ______________________________

____

c. ______________________________

____

1. What are the advantages of each alternative?
   a.______________________________
   b.______________________________
   c.______________________________

2. What are the disadvantages of each alternative?
   a.______________________________
   b.______________________________
   c.______________________________

3. How can you overcome these disadvantages?
   a.______________________________
   b.______________________________
   c.______________________________

Here is a table you can use to summarize your alternatives and get a quick overview.

FIND OVERLOOKED ALTERNATIVES

What are three alternative ways of solving the problem?		
Alternative 1	**Alternative 2**	**Alternative 3**
What are the advantages of each alternative?		
What are the disadvantages of each alternative?		
How can you overcome these disadvantages?		

1. Which of these three alternatives do you select to try?

____

____

____

2. Based on this alternative, what approach will you take to implement it?

____

____

____

3. Which of the five ill-logics do you need to correct to insure clear thinking in solving the problem?

____

____

____

4. What are the ways you can implement this approach?
   a.____

   ____

   b.____

   ____

   c.____

   ____

5. What obstacles could arise? How will you overcome them?

____

____

____

6. If your original plan doesn't work, what alternative will you use?

____

____

____

7. How will you reward yourself?

____

____

____

After completing these questions, discuss them with someone whose objectivity you trust. This fresh perspective could increase your skill and effectiveness in using the techniques.

CHAPTER 8

PAST PROBLEMS IN THE PRESENT

The Shadow and the Fly

Imagine yourself sitting comfortably in a sunny room, reading your favorite magazine. To your right is a large picture window. It looks out onto a garden. To your left is a large white wall. The sun's warm rays are streaming into the room, reflecting a slight glare from the wall.

From the corner of your eye you see something moving on the white wall. You glance up. The object moves, reverses its direction, then it jumps up to another spot. You become fascinated and fixed on that moving object on the wall. "What kind of bug is that?" you ask yourself. "I can't make it out."

What you don't realize is that the bug is not a bug. It's a shadow cast by a fly on the window pane of the picture window across the room. The shadow keeps "buzzing" around, flitting from here to there and back again.

Now this "bug" on the wall is distracting you from your relaxing reading. So you roll up the magazine in preparation for the kill. Slowly, carefully, you move into position in front of the wall. As you raise the magazine for the strike, the shadow moves. You move with it.

Strike now. Wham! Pow! Got you! Oops! Where is it? Over there. You were sure you got it. "What's going on here?" you muse.

The answer is, of course, you're chasing a shadow. The problem causing your distraction is not on the wall, but on the window. If we want to reduce the irritations and wasted effort because of stressful events and stressful people, then we need to make sure we are also dealing with the underlying problem—the old reaction —not just the shadow that's close at hand, the more obvious stressful event or stressful person.

Since old reactions camouflage themselves in present events and in present people, naturally the old reactions remain unrecognized. To solve the problems in our stressful events and with stressful people, and to avoid inflaming the stress, we need to recognize our old reactions and realize that they don't belong in the present.

Old Reactions in New Events

When they appear in the present, they intensify our stress and the original problem takes longer to solve. Even when the original problem gets solved, the effect of the old reaction can still leave us with residual stress. This secondary effect is also a problem and it needs to be addressed.

Triggers to Old Reactions

- Invasion of our territory or responsibilities
- Deadlines imposed by others
- Nonsupport from key people

- Being deprived of what we need or want
- Criticism of competency or integrity
- Failing and making mistakes
- Being blamed
- Unclear or excessive authority
- Contradictory expectations
- Win or lose, right or wrong competition
- Resistance and opposition
- Uncertainty and vague information
- Overload from too much work
- Non-communication (silent treatment)

Usually, there is a story behind each of our old reactions. To eliminate stress more quickly and thoroughly, we can deal with the reactions and the stories behind them. If we do not, our reaction will linger. It will keep us hot under the collar and limit our ability to feel stress-free from the problem.

Fortunately, current problems can be solved and stress dramatically reduced without totally eliminating old reactions. But after a problem is solved, there can be a nagging discontent from old reactions.

But with the mind free of old reactions, we can think more clearly and more quickly solve present problems. Here are some situations in which the past intrudes into the present.

The Case of the Boss Who Couldn't Be Pleased

Frank had a complaint. He couldn't seem to please his boss. After working hard on a proposal for a new procedure, he submitted it to the boss, only to find that the boss wanted the procedure to go in an entirely different direction. It was a very stressful event and the boss was becoming a very stressful person.

Frank was irritated and frustrated. "Why does he ask me to come up with new ideas, only to shoot them down?" he questioned. Two weeks later, Frank took the initiative to install another new method which would finish his project faster. The boss said that the new method was great but that Frank had applied it to the wrong project. There was a project that should have had higher priority.

"How can I second-guess him?" Frank wondered. He felt like he was chasing the boss's elusive approval. The more Frank pursued the boss's approval, the more disappointed Frank became. Frank's performance took a slide.

By defining his problem only around winning the boss's approval, Frank's chances of resolving it were limited. To confront the boss about his lack of approval would have dealt with only part of the problem anyway.

What remained unidentified was Frank's old reaction about uncertainty, vague objectives or vague information.

Frank can't stand uncertainty. Yet he is reluctant to find out what he needs to know. So he assumes that he understands what will please the boss. What Frank overlooked was obvious from the outside looking in. How can a project be completed to their mutual satisfaction without a prior meeting of the minds and without objectives being clearly understood?

Focusing on the approval issue distracted Frank from the old reaction. By mutually clarifying and setting objectives, Frank would know where he stands. Even if the boss remained stingy about vocalizing his approval, Frank's primary concern—uncertainty—would be quieted.

Frank's reaction and his reluctance to clarify was the past in the present. Frequently busy when Frank was a young boy, his father often was not available to clarify things. When he wanted Frank to do something, he made general requests, seldom giving clear directions. And when Frank would ask for more information, his father became impatient. "Stop asking so many questions" was his father's familiar refrain. "Figure things out for yourself" was his other pet expression.

As you can understand, it was not an easy matter for Frank to ask for clarification from his boss.

It takes just a little more effort to recognize that the old reactions are inflaming and confusing the current situation. What is important is identifying the complete picture and resolving the less obvious part of the problem.

The Case of Coworkers with an Attitude

Marilyn was sensitive about being in a nonsupport position from key people on whom she had to rely. On her new job, there were two women in particular in her work group from whom she needed support. If they didn't pass on timely information, were late with it, or inaccurate about it, her work was delayed or ineffective.

When no support happened the third time, Marilyn was furious. Part of her dismay was her belief that she looked bad in the eyes of the other people in her group. When she described the situation to her boss, it was difficult to solve the more objective information flow issues because Marilyn was so distracted by her reaction to no support.

After her meeting with her boss, Marilyn's conclusion was that the two offending members of the team had an attitude problem. She was sure they didn't care about the organization and that they were sloppy workers and self-centered people. Certainly, they were not team players, Marilyn thought, because when she confronted them with their mistakes and their untimely delivery of data, they assumed their attitude. They got defensive.

Clearly, Marilyn defined her problem around these people's attitude and aptitude. But this was not the only problem creating her stress.

Inflaming the situation was an old reaction—non-support from key people. This had its origins in her relationship with her younger brother and sister. Whenever her parents gave the three of them a job to do around the house, Marilyn wound up doing most of it, covering up for "the kids" who ran out to play after doing as little as possible. To make matters worse, if the project wasn't completed to her parents' satisfaction, she took all the blame.

During the next team meeting, Marilyn's two "adversaries" revealed that they felt she was hypercritical. And furthermore, she was only concerned about how she looked and making points with the boss and the group. They saw her as putting them down to build herself up.

The two women had their own old reactions. They perceived Marilyn as attacking their integrity and competence. They sensed her unstated evaluation of them as being uncaring, sloppy workers and not team players. Is it any wonder they were defensive and uncooperative in solving the information flow problem?

As it turned out, they could not fully participate in a clear thinking, problem-solving meeting to smooth out the work flow until they defined and reduced their sensitivities.

After two brief meetings, they cooled down and had insight into their own issues that were inflaming the situation. A few simple procedures were brainstormed that smoothed out the work flow. Though the work flow problem was resolved, there was still some carry over of the caution among them. In time, defensiveness and stress were reduced to a slight irritation—a reduction sufficient to keep the information flowing.

The Case of the Fence-Sitting In-Laws

Amanda's in-laws were visiting again. As usual, she did everything to please them. Despite Amanda's schedule that was already demanding—the kids, her new business, her husband's needs—she made herself available to entertain her in-laws. Although she loved them, they were driving her crazy. No matter what she did, no matter what she would ask, her in-laws could not make up their minds about where to go, what to do, or when to do it.

There was total vacillation.

Now, Amanda is a person who likes to make up her mind and take action. To her, backpedalling, mind-changing, and course-shifting are a waste of time, and time is especially precious when you have so much to do.

First, it was their arrival date. They changed the date three times. When they arrived in town, they decided to change hotels. The previous time Amanda spent getting them into the original hotel was wasted.

Amanda's husband had a seemingly more demanding schedule than she had—which seemed all too convenient for him—so that the burden of entertaining the in-laws fell on her shoulders until the weekend.

Now, with proper planning, she felt that she just might get all the entertaining accomplished, as well as her regular daily activities. Tough, but doable, she had thought to herself.

However, in practice, she kept getting caught in her in-laws' web of vacillation, making decisions and breaking decisions. It threw her planning off and began to immobilize Amanda. The more she tried to pin them down, the more frequent was their vacillation.

Amanda felt like a puppet on a string, and like being inside a maze with nothing but blind alleys.

One more mind-change and she would lose her composure. For a moment, she fantasized telling them in no uncertain terms, "Do it or forget it!"

What's the problem here? It's her in-laws' vacillation, of course.

Or is it?

So long as the problem was defined only as their vacillation, Amanda would remain all stressed up with no place to go.

In the brief time she had with them, she could not educate her in-laws to be more decisive, nor could she scold them for constantly pulling the rug out from under what she wanted to accomplish.

But Amanda's goal of demonstrating her competency and control over a challenging schedule—and still pleasing her in-laws—was being thwarted. She was experiencing their vacillation as resistance and opposition to what she wanted to accomplish.

Controlling her in-laws is a lost cause. How she reacts to resistance and opposition is not. But that is one of Amanda's old reactions.

For years, Amanda has had focus and purpose. Once she sets out on a course of action, nothing stands in her way. This was not always so. Growing up for Amanda was a restrictive experience, and she battled for every privilege allowed by her family. She had learned to mobilize her forces at a moment's opposition, and she could easily sense resistance no matter how slight.

Interestingly, control was also an issue for the in-laws. They appear to want to please Amanda as much as she wants to please them. But they are the kind of people who dislike being pinned down and who like to keep their options open. That's how they define control. They feel more in command by sitting on the fence and sliding off at the last minute. That way they can do what they wanted to do all along, or do at the last minute what seemed most advantageous.

Amanda, a direct, straight-ahead person, thought her in-laws lived in an 'alien' world. "How could anybody be so wishy-washy?" she asked herself. Do it or don't do it. That was Amanda's philosophy. If you do it and it doesn't work, then fix it. No harm done. All that's necessary, she believed, is the confidence to work yourself out of any situation.

Amanda's mother-in-law, putting some finishing touches to her makeup, turns to her husband. "Joe, do I look all right? I can't tell with this mirror."

"You look great. You're a winner, Sweetheart."

"Joe, how's my dress? Do you think it's too formal? Should I go casual?"

"Susan, I don't really know. You never can tell where they're taking us. You know what I mean? I feel like I'm on a tour. 'Go here, go there. Let's do this, let's do that.' I feel like we're in the hands of a social director. No, it's more like an army sergeant. I came here to relax, see the family, the kids. I'm happy to stay put!"

"Now, Joe, don't be so fussy. Let's go along with the 'program.' You know what I mean? Besides, I bought these new clothes. I want to get some use out of them."

Joe buttons up his gray cardigan. "Well, I just don't feel I fit in. Those fancy places are not for me. Do you suppose they're trying to impress us? You know, Mr. and Mrs. Success. In my day, I had plenty of opportunities, but I decided not to run myself into the ground. You watch, they're going to be in trouble if they keep up this pace.

"Joe, that's terrible. What would they think if they heard you?"

"Look, Susan, enough is enough. If they give us another timetable of events, tell them we have to think about it. Maybe they'll get the point and back off."

Joe feels imposed upon, herded into having a good time. He's feeling the time pressures, and there is a twinge of competition because he sees the "kids" as having more success. One of his old reactions is competition.

Another of Joe's reactions is overload—too many events in too short a time, for him. He feels overwhelmed. Plus there is some social overload—he's not comfortable in those "fancy places." Indirectly, he's getting pressure from his wife, too. She wants to go out often and go to the fine places where she can capitalize on her wardrobe.

These are the underlying problems of the in-laws' vacillation.

Beyond this, there is the reciprocal nature of their reactions: overload and competition for father-in-law, Joe, and resistance and opposition for Amanda. The more Joe reacts to being in overload with all the activity, the more opposition and resistance Amanda experiences from him. In her effort to manage her stress from the resistance, she pushes even harder and feeds her father-in-law's reaction to overload.

Despite their unspoken displeasure and judgments of each other, they are not wishy-washy in-laws and domineering "kids." They are typical people bouncing off each other's reactions, and they are only defining their stress by the visible, more obvious problems between them—vacillation and domination. This will not get it completely done until they recognize their lingering old reactions—resistance from others for her and overload for him.

As the above case histories illustrate, when we identify which yesteryear sensitivities from old reactions underlie our current behavior, we increase our understanding and objectivity about the present. It is then possible to diffuse and dissipate any lingering stress.

Part IV

How to Tolerate Relationships

CHAPTER 9

STRESS AND THE MYTH OF COMPATIBILITY

Four Patterns of Living and Loving

We often experience stress when we try to get what is most important to us—love. Why are so many people having difficulty getting and giving love? The paradox is that what we need the most—love—demands the knowledge and skills we possess the least. The search for love and sustaining it can be very stressful.

I can offer some solutions to this paradox, some skills to getting and giving love and, in the process, for experiencing less stress. We take the first step by understanding the limitations of the compatibility concept.

The Myth of Compatibility

Where is the perfect match? Somewhere out there! Mr. Right or Ms. Right can not be far away, nor can be the Right Boss, the Right Customers, the Right Patients, or the Right Life Partner. To search for them means a long, hard journey to nowhere.

This leads us through the mythical state of compatibility—where the ups and downs of seeking love creates more stress than the many hassles in other areas of our life and work.

Over and over, we hear people say, "You have to work at good relationships." Work at it? What kind of work? Where do we do it? When do we do it? Do we stand or sit? What tools do we use? Do we wear work clothes or our going-out best?

Sure, "work at it" people say—whatever that means. And if the relationship "isn't working," many want to "work it out." And if it doesn't work, then they move on—and start to work all over again.

If people elect to stay, or if they want to enrich the relationship, I can tell them what work has to be done and what the job entails.

Couples, Kaleidoscopes, and Compatibility

In looking at our relationships, we should view them as two beautiful, multicolored, twirling kaleidoscopes, side by side, trying to overlap and partially merge. The overlapping area of the two kaleidoscopes certainly should be no more than half of each kaleidoscope, or else one partner will lose individuality.

The kaleidoscopes must find room within the overlapping area to accommodate and synchronize each other's multicolored pieces to form a new pattern. It takes time to synchronize all these pieces, which represent our behaviors, values, goals, priorities, and preferences.

Over time, they may collide rather than find a smooth space to interlace. The pieces may grind and chip, occasionally breaking and jamming the kaleidoscopes.

Universally, there are only four human kaleidoscopes that represent our basic patterns of living, working, and loving. As I have indicated before, I call these patterns Controlling, Supporting, Conserving, and Adapting. While each of us has some capacity for all four patterns, most of us favor one or two. Since childhood, we have learned which patterns work best for us and we generally follow these patterns throughout our life.[2]

All four patterns are found in both sexes. No gender has a monopoly on any pattern or the philosophy of life underlying it.

Basic Patterns of Living and Loving

As you read the capsule descriptions below, decide which patterns are most like you and your partner.

Controlling Pattern

A successful life comes from seizing opportunity, being competent. Acting quickly, focusing on end results

---

[2] *Name of Your Game,* Dr. Stuart Atkins, 2002, 2nd ed., Business Consultants, Inc., available through The Schutz Company, New York. www.poweredbylifo.com.

and directing others will make things happen. Staying competitive and confident leads to success and exciting love.

Lisa prefers the Controlling way of living and loving. The wooing and winning are key satisfactions. Feeling in charge of the relationship is also an important requirement if the relationship is to continue.

For Lisa, passion and excitement are the goal. But her intense love burns brightly until the novelty wanes. Then there is a sudden doubt. Is it love after all? If it is love, then why is the flame flickering?

She gives little thought to the impossibility of such sustained passion. Nevertheless, Lisa might try to distance herself from her partner. That way she can have the ecstasy of reuniting, of kissing and making up, of going through the cycle again and again. Sometimes the ups and downs are with the same person. Sometimes it is with the added novelty of a new partner.

Lisa wants surprises and unpredictability in the relationship, anything to keep it from becoming routine. She will expect enthusiasm and excitement from her partner.

In this way of loving, there can be contradictory needs. On the one hand, there can be the desire for someone who will have the vitality and spirit to spar on an equal basis, stand up for themselves, and spark off energy to fuel the intensity. On the other hand, there can be the need for her partner to be supportive, nurturing and a good follower.

There is also an underlying premise in this pattern, "I can take all that you want to give, and when my needs are filled, I will be free and generous in giving you what you need.

Supporting Pattern

A successful life comes from hard work and always trying harder. Try to do the very best; set high standards for yourself and others. There is the pursuit of excellence, even though nothing or nobody requires it. Be thoughtful, trusting, giving, and loyal, then lasting love will naturally follow.

Joe loves with his heart and mind. He is filled with ideal expectations, high hopes, promises of loyalty, and long-term commitment. Love is togetherness. Love is forever.

Giving his time and attention, doing many things for his partner, this is his way of sustaining love. But at times, he gives too much and that can trigger in his partner feelings of being overwhelmed and indebted for the generosity. Sometimes that sense of obligation can make his partner feel distant and resentful for not being able to measure up to that standard of giving.

Joe is also admiring and adoring. Trust and belief are freely given, but if his partner fails to live up to the trust, then feelings of disappointment or betrayal emerge. When there is a loss of innocence and illusion, the fall is disheartening. It takes a long time to re-establish trust. Time is also needed to push out the hurt and heal the wounds of unfilled promises.

Underlying all of this is a basic love premise: To get love, I have to give it. I hope to be rewarded in kind for my loving acts, but if I give more than I get, I'll gladly make the sacrifice for love.

Conserving Pattern

A successful life comes from making the most of what we have, being factual and rational, using our head to control our heart. Be methodical, logical, precise, and tenacious. Before acting, try to analyze every angle; look always for the fail-safe way to do things. Be practical, reserved and take love one step at a time, being careful not to get too involved too soon before there is a high degree of certainty in the relationship.

Kay prefers a calm, cool, and collected love. She doesn't think there is much sense in wallowing in sentimentality and emotional fantasies. She believes that if you keep your feet on the ground, the relationship can take its natural course. There's no sense in rushing things. By using her head, Kay thinks that she will ensure a lasting and solid relationship based on reality and reason.

Because there is a quiet reserve in this way of loving, it is easy to assume that her love does not run deep. Though there may be fewer clear, overt acts, her feeling for her partner may be intense. Only the expression of the feelings may be difficult. But the expressions of love surface in many practical acts of caring. Doing everyday things has considerable meaning when they reflect care and love.

At times, because the expressions of love are indirect and practical, the love can be overlooked or misunderstood. Her partner may want some sentimental, or playful display of emotion and affection. But this is not likely to frequently happen.

The underlying premise in loving is, if we take things a step at a time our relationship will deepen as we go. By taking it slowly but surely, we can build our relationship on a solid foundation.

Adapting Pattern

A successful life comes from pleasing others, filling their needs first. Getting to know people and getting along is important. Be flexible, enthusiastic, tactful and charming. Try to display sensitivity and empathy toward partner and smooth over difficulties and problems as soon as possible.

For Mark, doing things and going places together is a big part of the partnership. Playing together and having fun often covers his underlying seriousness. Being casual and off-handed hides his vulnerability and concern about losing other people's approval or love.

Pleasing others is his main motive for action. He is willing to do many things to keep his partner happy. No effort is too large or small if it pleases. Often Mark's efforts will be dramatized to make sure his partner gets the message.

Despite feelings of anger or discontent, his actions can appear enthusiastic and happy-go-lucky. He uses the light touch of humor to soothe, even when the gaiety can be concealing hurt or worry about the relationship.

If there is a lover's quarrel, he will make a quick attempt to patch things up or make amends. As a result, some vital issues about his relationship may not be given a sufficient airing. Issues and problems can pop up continuously because they may have been hurriedly smoothed over.

When his partner's spirits are low, Mark will make an effort to pick up the mood. He will be concerned that harmony is slipping away, and he will make an attempt to rescue his partner from any bad feelings which could break the harmony and upset the relationship. The underlying premise in loving this way is, live, love and be happy.

Take a moment to consider the four patterns and answer the following questions:

Which pattern(s) are most like you?

____

____

Which are most like your partner?

____

____

Which pattern(s) is least like you?

____

____

Which pattern(s) is least like your partner?

____

____

Which pattern is difficult to understand?

____

____

Why?

___

___

In the early stages of the relationship, couples are immersed in the novelty and passion of their situation. Each partner's behavior patterns are perceived but discounted, or ignored. *Romantic love is a temporary pact to suspend reality.*

When romantic love and its excitement begin to wear off, differences begin to emerge and so the need for power comes into focus. "My way" versus "your way" takes center stage. Then begins the strenuous process of blending living habits, priorities, values, likes and dislikes, along with patterns of living and loving.

These core interactions are played out during disagreements over the little, day-to-day problems or once-in-a-while crisis.

Little and Big Problems That Create Stress

It is around occasional big problems and daily little ones that the relationship is tested. In trying to resolve these problems, the partners will interact with their own characteristic behavior patterns.

Typical Problems—Little Ones

Going out or staying at home

Going out with my friends or your friends

Going out with one couple or several couples

Seeing the action movie or the love story
Seeing your parents or mine
Driving too fast or too slow
Sleeping with the windows open or shut
Having sex daily or on the weekend
Making the room too hot or too cold
Eating out or eating in
Serving the salad before the main meal or with it
Cleaning up dishes now or later
Fixing the fence or painting the bedroom
Buying a new couch or a new TV
Listening to my problems or yours

Typical Problems—Big Ones

Out of work
Change in work hours
Passed over for promotion
Savings ran out
Moving
Death of a family member
Conflict with parents
Divorcing previous partner
Ex-husband, ex-wife, ex-sweetheart
Too many bills
Not enough money
Being sued
Illness
Accident
Birth of a child

Often the big problems create so much stress that the little ones become exaggerated in importance. Sometimes the little problems get eclipsed by the larger ones. Even when there are no big problems, the minor annoyances provide a large field to play out the stress of having similar or different behavior patterns.

No matter what causes a fight between partners, what makes it difficult to resolve are the basic behavior patterns—Controlling, Supporting, Conserving, Adapting. They determine how we fight, compromise, set priorities and make decisions in resolving the big and little problems.

Which is Better—Having the Same or Different Patterns?

Some questions naturally arise when considering these patterns. Which patterns are compatible? Is it less stressful when you are similar to or different from the other person? Do people with opposites patterns get along better, or do people who are alike?

The answer is neither. It makes no difference if you are the same or different. There are advantages and disadvantages to both. The question should be, "How can we deal with the relationship problems that arise from having similar or different behavior patterns?

Compatibility, therefore, is less about finding the right person and more about dealing with the implications of being the same or different. Notwithstanding our original common interests and physical attractions, if the relationship is to last, we have to work on the inevitable and universal problems that stem from our basic behavior patterns.

As a result, a relationship is a work in progress. It gets better or it gets worse. There is no final product, only a better product. It is fostered by the pleasures of companionship and sex, and forged by the courage to fight and compromise in the service of improving the work in progress—the relationship.

But fighting is fun for one, frightening for another. Some of us fight for principles. Some of us fight with facts. Some fight at the drop of a hat.

After a fight comes compromise. Each of us has our own way to resolve differences through some kind of give and take. With the Controlling pattern, it is more take and less give. Supporting is more give and less take. Conserving is give-a-little, take-a-little. And the Adapting pattern is give now, take later.

Four Patterns of Fighting and Making Up

Below are descriptions of how people with each of the four basic patterns fight and compromise.

Controlling Pattern

Fighting

Donna is quick to defend her territory and prerogatives. She is firm and very clear about where she stands. She comes on so strong at times that she can be experienced as demanding or arrogant. Her partner can feel coerced. Donna can be so quick to protect her rights and interests from exploitation that sometimes she's defensive and ready to argue over the slightest suggestion of unfairness.

In a dispute, she finds it difficult to let up until the air is cleared. This can create an intense atmosphere, making others feel under the third degree as she presses and probes for answers. Her partner can sometime feel there's no breathing room.

Compromising

For Donna, compromise equals a hard bargain, a competitive give and take. The only worthy adversary for her is one who will wrestle through to a compromise, staying in the contest every inch of the way. She just can't respect backing down or giving in. Rather, Donna admires and appreciates sparring on an equal basis through the whole negotiation.

She is more prone to compromise when a solution is urgently needed and time is running out; or when there is a chance of losing an opportunity. If the compromise centers around who is going to be in charge, as it frequently will, then responsibility should be divided, providing separate areas of autonomy.

Supporting Pattern

Fighting

When discussions get hot and heavy, Hal is willing to extend himself to do what he sees as right and fair. Because he feels a commitment to establishing cooperation, he can be vulnerable to giving in. All too often, he can make too many concessions.

Sometimes Hal can get moralistic or self-righteous. He can make his partner feel guilty by conveying that he is a victim of injustice. He can display hurt, disappointment, or downright martyrdom to get his way.

Compromising

Compromise is possible with Hal if it does not violate his principles. If he sees the solution to a problem as fair and just to all concerned, then compromise is acceptable. The needs of others are a vital concern, and if he sees his partner as needy, he will give in.

In seeking a solution to a disagreement, a satisfactory compromise may not be enough for him. In compromise, as in other activities, he must find the very best solution possible, one which reflects the highest principles and purpose.

Conserving Pattern

Fighting

With John, the byword is tenacity. By sticking to his guns he demonstrates conviction. But his partner can experience him as unbending, or stubborn. In fighting, John tries to be reasonable by relying heavily on facts to document his position.

When the atmosphere becomes emotional, John tends to wait until cooler heads prevail. Because of this waiting period, it may appear that he doesn't care. He can become aloof and distant, not giving his partner the satisfaction of sustained effort or the satisfaction that he has been influenced by his partner's opposing position.

Compromising

John thinks logic and reason are the pathways to compromise. In working to find a solution to disagreement, he considers all the alternatives and thoroughly explores them. With him, compromises should be implemented in phases. After a successful small step, then larger steps can be taken.

By keeping emotions at a low level with facts, John helps to ensure that the situation doesn't get out of hand. He uses rules of order and a well constructed outline or agenda to serve as a map, helping to navigate through the troubled waters.

Adapting Pattern

Fighting

When Ann is involved in a fight, harmony is her overall concern. As a result, she is willing to understand and weigh both sides of the argument, to find a mutually satisfactory solution. But after a while, this can lead to vacillation and inconsistency, confusing her partner about where she stands on the issues.

During a disagreement, she makes an effort to smooth things out quickly, and to keep the tension low through humor. This prevents her objections from being fully expressed, and so the air is not cleared. Then the problem will reappear at a later time. She needs encouragement to disagree.

Compromising

Ann's motto is that everybody can win in a compromise. This prevents people from feeling like unhappy losers. She believes that winning at somebody else's expense just sets up a personal contest which will appear repeatedly during future disagreements. And she doesn't think winning should become more important than finding a compromise.

In a disagreement, Ann is willing to go along and make amends, this time, in the service of getting along. Keeping the action flowing is important to her, so she looks for a solution that will keep everybody happy. Ann doesn't want disagreement to develop into a running battle. She is always open to new ways to overcome an impasse, demonstrating her flexibility.

So these are the ways in which we fight and compromise, each in our own way. How quickly we deal with our similarities and differences in our behavior patterns, how quickly we do the "work" necessary for our combined patterns will determine how quickly we resolve our disagreements and minimize our stress.

CHAPTER 10

COUPLE PATTERNS AND RELATIONSHIP STRESS

Attractions, Problems, and Solutions

One of the attractions of having the same pattern is the familiarity with each other's ways. It gives us an illusion of compatibility and the expectation of less stress. What is more, priorities and preferences may be clearly understood. In some ways, it is like looking into a mirror and seeing some of our own behavior reflected back to us.

Being Alike—Problems and the Work To Be Done

This mirror reflection stresses us because we would just as soon forget about some of what we see. We are not proud of some behaviors—usually some of our excesses—and do not want to be reminded of them. To distract ourselves, we usually become critical of our partner's similar behavior, acting as if we never do that!

Consider now the following combinations of similar patterns, particularly the problems that inevitably and universally arise, and the work that needs to be done on the relationships.

Special Instructions

If you and your partner have similar patterns, you can choose to only read about that similar pattern combination and skip the others. If you and your partner do not have similar patterns, you may want to skip to the explanation of different pattern combinations. This chapter is organized in such a way that you can use it as a reference for a past, current, or future relationship.

Same Pattern

Controlling and Controlling .... page 169
Supporting and Supporting .... page 171
Conserving and Conserving .... page 173
Adapting and Adapting .... page 175

Different Patterns

Supporting and Controlling.................................. page 178
Supporting and Conserving.................................. page 180
Supporting and Adapting...................................... page 183
Controlling and Conserving .... page 185
Controlling and Adapting .... page 187
Conserving and Adapting .... page 190

If you would like to compare the patterns of all couples, then read ahead. Reading all the descriptions can provide contrasts to sharpen your understanding of your own relationship. But you can use the chapter only as a reference for a current relationship.

Controlling and Controlling

Problems from This Combination

When this couple disagrees, the sparks can fly. If they get too invested in their opinion or position, disagreements can escalate to arguments to fiery clashes. After a cooling off period, some brief bitterness turns to sweetness as they kiss and make up, forgive and forget—until the next time.

Every so often they will ask each other, "Who made you the boss of this relationship?" They have little tolerance for domination. The lack of tolerance is such that genuine attempts to give advice and help will be experienced as control and domination, the good intentions completely overlooked.

Occasionally, in a moment of distraction, because of resentment or capriciousness, one of the partners will act unilaterally on something they want very much. To avoid serious consequences, the unilaterally acting partner knows that a strong, persuasive case must be built to convince the other to agree to the self-serving action. How out of control the other partner feels in areas outside the relationship will determine whether the persuasion persuades.

If the selling effort proves ineffective, then there will be recriminations all delivered in one breath, "You insist that I consult you on every decision, but you don't have to consult me, is that it? You have a double standard, my friend. That was a selfish thing to do. If that's the name of the game, two can play it—watch me!"

Some minutes, hours, in some cases, days later, the offending partner evens the score in a positive way.

Some special individual benefit is offered to bring the relationship back into parity—a gift, or some activity promised but long delayed because of procrastination.

The Work That Needs To Be Done

The "work" this couple has to do centers on the balance of power. Dividing the major responsibilities in the relationship is essential. Each has to have a territory of their own in which a final decision is theirs to make. This does not mean they cannot consult with each other, but going in, they can feel comfortable knowing that, a priori, one of them is clearly in charge here.

In my relationship with my wife regarding our home, I am in charge of all landscaping decisions and my wife has the say-so on interior design and decorating. The power rests heavy with us, not wanting to do anything that would make it unpleasant for someone we love so much. We go overboard in consulting with each other despite our prearranged power. Knowing the power is there seems to quiet the need to use it.

At the psychological level, I am in charge of all improvements in the relationship and she is in charge of being right. I point the way to what we need to do to improve our life and love, and she determines if it is right or wrong. If there is strong disagreement over what or who is right or wrong, she prevails since she is in charge of that.

As a result, I get to recommend an alternative improvement, and usually on the second try, she does not invoke her right-or-wrong power.

Another work area for this combination has to do with overload—too many things going on at the same time. With the compounding of the Controlling/ Controlling couple's energy, their need for activity and accomplishment, they become time poor and many things are in various stages of incompletion. Establishing clear cut priorities is a must, and then following through on them is mandatory. Trying to do everything at once puts the relationship under avoidable stress.

Lastly, taking more time to be together is crucial. Be it an evening, a day or a weekend, they need chances to reconnect at an intimate level. And with such emphasis on doing in the relationship, they occasionally need to do nothing with each other. It can be immensely renewing if they can stand the singular activity of doing nothing. Being so active, however, after a while they can find several new ways of doing nothing!

Supporting and Supporting

Problems from This Combination

With both partners having such high standards and expectations for themselves, there can be considerable stress, disappointment and bitterness if they fall short of their ideals.

Another problem with this combination is that striving for total togetherness at the extreme can be debilitating and depressing. With such closeness, there can be a loss of individuality and one's own identity. Here, so to speak, the two kaleidoscopes overlap so much that what should be three beautiful, dynamic patterns compress to one. The richness and variation is diminished, and there are so many shapes and colors to synchronize that the resulting pattern is sluggish. Action is sacrificed for mutuality and oneness.

Each has a strong need to be helpful, not only in their own relationship, but with most friends, relatives and coworkers. Often they become overcommitted to helping people, putting out extra effort and time. They are ambivalent about the time each gives to other people. On the one hand, they admire each other for their generosity with people who need their help. On the other hand, they are both bothered by each others' stress from trying too hard and doing too much with too many people. And ironically, they might be a bit jealous of all the time and energy the partner is spending on others.

Being so thoughtful of each other, being so helpful to other people, can leave each with the feeling that they are neglecting themselves. When finally there is some minor falling out, each will be thinking, "After all I've done, after all I've given, this is my thanks?!"

There can be covert competition in the relationship. It is expressed through trying to outdo each other in helping and giving to each other. This is a subtle form of "potlatch," an old Indian custom of trying to outdo the other by giving bigger and more beautiful gifts. Another form of competition can be that "my principles are more principled than your principles."

The Work That Needs To Be Done

Ironically, because there is so much focus on giving, the partners can feel depleted and deprived. The work they need to do for the relationship and for themselves is to evolve a better balance of giving and receiving.

Though they receive much satisfaction in giving, they need more often to be the recipient of their own giving.

They need to selfishly help themselves and take care of their other needs, besides their need to give.

Setting limits and learning how to say "No" to people who ask for help will make time for self-help and time for the relationship.

Other work of this relationship involves in setting more realistic expectations and standards. Developing an ideal relationship, being the best they can be, is inspiring and lofty, as long as it is not unattainable. Excellence is their goal, but if it is pushed to perfection, they are headed for a fall. When they fail to reach perfection, they will try harder and put even greater stress on their relationship.

They need to be more forgiving of their frailties and foibles. They need to be less critical of themselves and ease up on their standards.

Finally, their work is to become more independent of each other, and be different and daring inside the relationship with a minimum loss of mutuality. Then they can have the safety and satisfaction of a loving relationship without submerging their individuality.

As a result, the overlapping area of their merging kaleidoscopes will be better defined, and their own areas will have their own unique movement.

Conserving and Conserving

Problems from This Combination

One of the problems these lovers face is analysis paralysis. In searching for alternatives and trade-offs, they can become immobilized while weighing their options. Their plans can be so complex, with many variations and variables, that the plans are difficult to implement, leaving them happy with the plan but frustrated because there is little accomplishment.

Another problem comes from their reluctance to throw things out until they are well used and beyond. Consequently, things seem to pile up, things they do not need now, but may need sometime in the near or distant future.

When they have disagreements, the Conserving/ Conserving couple present their position, arguments, and evidence—politely taking turns. They do not like to raise their voices and hope to reason their way to agreement. After each states their case, they back off hoping the other will appreciate the logic and evidence they have presented. Quietly, they wait for the other to see the light and come around to their point of view.

This can sometimes lead to a stalemate if not a checkmate. During this period, the relationship climate can become chilly and cool with formality. In the meantime, they are busy digging in behind their respective walls. They cut themselves off from love and other positive feelings, as they review in their mind the incontrovertible wisdom of their own logic.

Who will make the first move toward turning a meeting of the minds into a meeting of the hearts? Who will dare peek over the wall while waving the white flag of love? The partner who feels the least rejected and the most secure will acknowledge seeing some of the logic—finally—in the other's position.

The Work That Needs To Be Done

There is a work plan for these Conserving partners for future arguments. The plan consists of three rules. First, seek third-party arbitration as soon as the walls go up. This can take the form of facts in articles, books, or other information sources. Second, keep in contact. Retreating from each other should be considered a time out, lasting no longer than one hour. And third, the first statement by either partner after the time out should be, "Loving you is more important to me than being right."

Time limits, in general, are important for them. This will help them counteract their natural bent toward being overelaborate and prone to analysis paralysis. Setting deadlines and sticking to them can limit their time in planning and problem solving. An imperfect, timely decision is better than a perfect one after the need has past.

The final work this couple must try is to enrich their facts with feelings. Sticking to the hard facts ignores the fact that feelings are facts, facts about our emotional state. This is important information for them to share if they are to improve their communication.

Adapting and Adapting

Problems from This Combination

These partners feel that after they have accommodated so much to please the other, my partner "owes me." There's a private ledger kept on which all credits for pleasing are recorded. "Since I did something for you, now it's your turn to do something for me." It's quid pro quo, something for something. Each thinks,

"We'll take turns, only you come first, as long as you give me what I need in turn later on."

When the Adapting partners finally ask for something and are turned down, they can feel hurt and anger because their markers were not honored, the IOU's were not paid. Surprisingly, they are unaware that each is keeping score and has an expectation that the marker will be honored.

With this Adapting behavior, stress is handled by striving to keep tension low, getting things done through a humorous approach, and smoothing things out with reassuring promises and staying positive. The other side of this, the excess, is that they can distract themselves from the seriousness of a situation, and they may raise hopes too high with their enthusiasm and optimism.

When they want to express some dissatisfaction, their tact and diplomacy can boomerang. In an effort to lighten up their request for a change in their partner's behavior, the impact of their statements is neutralized by their finesse. In effect, the message is so softened and camouflaged that it is unrecognizable. Their light touch, their humor, also distracts from the seriousness of their need and dissipates their impact. They are not taken seriously because they do not sound serious.

As a result, there are some issues that do not get fully talked about and resolved. These appear and reappear as a continuous cycle in the course of the relationship. After a while, both wonder, "Why don't we do something about it?" They are doing something about it—they are avoiding it and the quality of their relationship!

The Work That Needs To Be Done

The work here is for both of them to be more direct. When they have a disagreement, they need to stay with it until they can clear the air by putting more thoughts, facts, and feelings on the problem solving table. To help them do this, they have to face their fear of alienating one another and losing approval.

Since this is a tough task, a specific time must be scheduled in a serious setting. This is a stretch for this couple, because their usual behavior is informal and spontaneous without rules, regulations, or restrictions. But a serious atmosphere is a must. If they get in an informal or casual atmosphere, they are most likely to avoid tackling this uncomfortable discussion by being playful and funny.

This Adapting behavior can eventually lead them astray, causing them to lose sight of their own goals, by trying to facilitate the goals of the other. Therefore, it takes them longer to complete things. By the time they return to their own agenda, the timeliness may have passed or their energy may have waned or their learning curve may have slipped. It can cost time, love, or money—maybe all three.

Whether they over-facilitate each other, or people outside the relationship, the same remedial approach applies. "Go first and stay with it." My recommendation is don't allow yourself to be pulled off course by the lure of approval. This "work" will improve relationships. By filling more of your own needs first, it will head off the resentment that can come from playing second fiddle while the other person goes first.

Up till now, I have described the problems of having the same behavior patterns as your partner, and the work to be done to improve the relationship. Now consider what happens when partners have different patterns.

Being Different—Attractions, Problems, and the Work To Be Done

One of the advantages of having different behavior patterns is the opportunity to learn from the differences. Even though these differences can be stressful, they offer an expanded perspective on problems and offer new possibilities to act in novel and enriching ways.

A paradox exists between partners who have different patterns. What attracts them to each other about the other's pattern is the same thing that frustrates them and is a major source of tension—especially when the other perceives the behavior as excessive.

Each partner has to learn to see the connection between the pattern benefits they like and the inevitable problems the pattern causes. Accepting this paradox makes it easier to do the work that needs to be done to deal with the paradox. This is in the service of getting more satisfaction and less tension in the relationship.

Supporting–Controlling

Attractions

The partner who prefers the Supporting pattern is excited by the drive, forcefulness and confidence of the partner who prefers the Controlling pattern. The Supporting partner likes the energy and intensity that the Controlling partner brings to the relationship and appreciates how the active, results-oriented approach can help make dreams come true and lofty ideals become concrete.

If the Supporting partner becomes too involved in taking care of the needs of people outside the relationship, he or she can count on the Controlling partner to ask, "What's in it for you, for us?" and to help extricate the Supporting partner from the bonds of social obligations.

The partner who prefers the Controlling pattern is pleased by the thoughtfulness, helpfulness, and receptivity of the Supporting partner. He or she finds comfort in the lack of competitiveness and the willingness of the Supporting partner to let the Controlling partner make decisions and take the lead. The Supporting partner provides a welcomed relief from the rough-and-tumble workaday world and restores the Controlling partner's equilibrium and energies as no one else can.

Problems

The major problems in a relationship between Supporting and Controlling partners arise over conflicts between doing what is right and doing what is expedient to get results. The Supporting partner wants to make sure that everyone's needs are taken into consideration, while the Controlling partner simply wants something and wants it now.

The Supporting partner can see the Controlling partner as overbearing, ruthless, unprincipled, and overly demanding. The Controlling partner can see the Supporting partner as too needy, not action-oriented enough, and too soft. Their arguments usually boil down to dreams vs. reality, doing your very best vs. just doing to get fast results.

The Work That Needs To Be Done

When conflict arises between these partners, the Supporting partner needs to become more practical and to recognize that his or her helpful thoughts and dreams won't help anyone unless they are acted upon. The Supporting partner needs to lower his or her standards of judgment and appreciate that, although the Controlling partner may do things a little too quickly and imperfectly, at least things get done.

When communicating with his or her partner, the Supporting partner needs to speak less about what is right and fair and more about what can be done and how quickly. The Controlling partner needs to push less and to first make sure the action addresses the standards of the other and has a worthwhile, relevant purpose.

Supporting–Conserving

Attractions

The partner who prefers the Supporting pattern is attracted to the steadfast commitment of the partner who prefers the Conserving pattern. He or she knows that the Conserving partner's love is strong, deep and constant. The Supporting partner also feels great security in the knowledge that his or her partner will take good care of all that they have together and won't jeopardize their relationship by doing anything foolish or impulsive. The Supporting partner is also attracted to the way in which the Conserving partner's practicality, openness to reason and planning can help make a vision for a better future, one step at a time.

The partner who prefers the Conserving pattern appreciates the idealism and commitment to excellence that the Supporting partner quietly lives out in his or her daily life. The Conserving partner is grateful for the Supporting partner's loyalty, helpfulness, and patience. The Supporting partner's vision of how things could and should be provides a welcome inspiration that helps to lift the Conserving partner's vision out of the habitual routines and mundane pursuits of daily life, offering rewarding new possibilities and alternatives.

Problems

Difficulties in this relationship often arise over conflict between the Supporting partner's desire toward selfless giving and the Conserving partner's concern to hold onto what they have. When these difficulties arise, the Supporting partner wants to do the right thing. But out of a sense of obligation and commitment to the relationship, the Supporting partner may swallow some feelings, carrying on as best as he or she can, all the while fueling the fire of mutual resentment with unspoken and spoken judgments.

The Supporting partner can see the Conserving partner as too cautious, too tied down to ritual and habit, and not feeling or caring enough about people. He or she can feel intense loneliness, sorrowful that his or her ideals and aspirations go unappreciated and sometimes even actively resisted.

The Conserving partner can, in turn, see the Supporting partner as too emotional and impractical. He or she can get frustrated by the Supporting partner's dreaminess and utopian fantasies. The Conserving partner, wanting to keep his or her feet firmly planted on the ground, can see the Supporting partner as lost in the clouds, drifting from one unrealistic reverie to another. He or she can respond by becoming withdrawn, resistant, and unemotional. Together, these partners can settle into a dutiful routine of daily living from which real love gradually drains away, leaving only a dry shell where once an intense love united them.

The Work That Needs To Be Done

To restore the richness of this relationship, the Supporting partner needs to judge less and to love more. He or she needs to recognize the hidden harshness in his or her own standards and realize that they sometimes block achievement of the very ideals that he or she strives to bring into being. Instead of finding fault, criticizing, and arguing over whose way is the right or best way, he or she needs to communicate clearly and rationally about his or her own needs, and express appreciation for the Conserving partner's capacity to take care of practical details and to make things work in the real world.

The Conserving partner needs to make a greater effort to express his or her real feelings, rather than just ideas or opinions. He or she needs to let go and learn to give some things away without considering it a loss. He or she needs to dream a little, to wish a little, to entertain at least a few fantasies about what could be instead of concentrating on what has been or what is most practical.

The Conserving partner needs to assure the Supporting partner that he or she deeply values the Supporting partner's helpfulness and desire to contribute something of lasting value to the world.

Supporting–Adapting

Attractions

The partner who prefers the Supporting pattern is attracted to the cheerfulness and good humor of the partner who prefers the Adapting pattern. He or she finds the Adapting partner's lightheartedness and flexibility a welcome relief from his or her own tendency towards excessive seriousness. The Adapting partner's openness, enthusiasm for whatever happens, and animated spontaneity, are welcomed as a light touch to contrast the seriousness of the Supporting partner's concerns for everybody's happiness and well-being.

The partner who prefers the Adapting pattern loves the thoughtfulness and cooperative spirit of the partner who prefers the Supporting pattern. He or she also appreciates the way in which the Supporting partner's vision for a better life together gives direction, purpose, and depth to their relationship. He or she likes the Supporting partner's receptivity to his or her spontaneous impulses and feels safe and secure because of the Supporting partner's unquestioned loyalty.

Problems

This relationship can suffer from both partners trying too hard to be nice. The danger arises because they do it in such different ways and are liable to misread each others' intentions. The Supporting partner can see the

Adapting partner's desire to "go along to get along" as a lack of moral fiber, as insincere and superficial. He or she wants deep and honest encounters about truly important issues, but at times he or she can see the Adapting partner as flippant and committed to little more than fun and games.

On the other hand, the Adapting partner feels dragged down by the Supporting partner's seriousness. He or she can quickly tire of the Supporting partner's idealism and altruism, wanting to know "What's in it for me?" When things get rough, he or she wants to help by lightening things up, by having a good time, by breezing over the troubles, and just maybe by poking fun at the Supporting partner's piousness. He is distressed when the Supporting partner becomes offended and critical and may flee even further into fun and games—either within or outside of the relationship.

The Work That Needs To Be Done

To ensure that this relationship will survive rocky times, the Supporting partner needs to understand that the Adapting partner's flexibility and willingness to accommodate expresses a strong desire to be liked and appreciated.

Because of this, the Supporting partner needs to refrain from criticizing or sounding judgmental. Instead, the Supporting partner needs to consistently and repeatedly express approval and support of the Adapting partner's ideas and facilitating actions.

The Adapting partner, on the other hand, needs to take the Supporting partner more seriously. He or she needs to stop playing, at least for a little while, and try to understand the important issues that are of such consequence to the Supporting partner.

The Adapting partner needs to minimize coloring unpleasant information as if it were pleasant. This partner needs to avoid glossing over unpleasant facts as a way of keeping harmony and minimizing conflict. Most important, he or she needs to recognize that the Supporting partner will express love when the deepest and truest emotions, wishes, and desires are openly shared.

Controlling–Conserving

Attractions

The partner who prefers the Conserving pattern is attracted to the intense energy, excitement, and initiative of the partner who prefers the Controlling pattern. The Controlling partner offers stimulation, variety, and change, and the assurance that things will get done quickly.

If the Conserving partner is moving too cautiously or analyzing things too much, he or she can count on the Controlling partner to liven things up with a sense of urgency to act, to get things done, to move on to the next thing.

The partner who prefers the Controlling pattern is attracted to the evenness, stability, and thoroughness of the Conserving partner. The Conserving partner acts as a weighted keel for the relationship, keeping everything on course whether they are in smooth or stormy waters. One feels security, safety, and a sense of permanence in the presence of a Conserving partner.

Problems

The biggest conflicts between these two patterns usually arise over two issues: timing and thoroughness. The Controlling partner likes to make quick decisions after a minimum of reflection. He or she wants to act now, and is already on to the next thing while the Conserving partner is still savoring what's now. The Conserving partner may feel that he or she has not had enough time to think about an issue, or has insufficient information to make a sound decision. He or she may see the Controlling partner as too impulsive, too emotional, and too much of a risk taker. On the other hand, the Controlling partner may get impatient at the Conserving partner's slow and steady pace. He or she may feel that the Conserving partner is too slow to react, bogged down with trivial details, and overly cautious. He or she may feel frustrated that the Conserving partner is curbing what he or she wants to do.

The Work That Needs To Be Done

To make this relationship prosper, the Controlling partner needs to exhibit more patience, so he or she can honor the Conserving partner's need to evaluate multiple options before making a decision and to take action one step at a time. The Controlling partner needs to provide more detailed information about what he or she is thinking and doing, and needs to assure the Conserving partner that nothing important will be done without checking first.

In times of stress or conflict, the Controlling partner needs to back off, to stop pushing, and be less demanding and commanding. He or she needs to express appreciation for the other partner's contribution of thinking through the important details and to making the most of what they have built up together.

In contrast, the Conserving partner needs to develop a higher tolerance for risk, for change, for the unknown and the unexpected. When there is conflict, instead of emotionally withdrawing, becoming stubborn, gathering facts and finding logical reasons to win the argument, he or she needs to get straight to the point, and express a willingness to compromise more. A show of feelings, and regard for the Controlling partner, will balance the use of facts and logic.

In addition, the Conserving partner needs to allow the Controlling partner to feel more in control and needs to explain the importance of the plans and alternatives provided, so that in the long run, they will get more of what they want if they defer action until the plan is solid.

Controlling–Adapting

Attractions

Action, directness, and results impress the Adapting partner. Also admired is the way in which the Controlling partner moves ahead with the goal in mind and with much less concern about gaining other people's approval.

From the point of view of the Controlling partner, the Adapting pattern has its merits. Often the Adapting partner will take the strain and tension out of a situation with humor and flexibility. This willingness to go along, to compromise, helps the Controlling partner feel more in charge.

In this couple, there is a mutual appreciation of their spontaneity, the plans made at the last minute and the sudden change of plans if their mood swings in another direction.

The Adapting partner likes the sense of urgency and the fast pace of the Controlling partner, along with the forcefulness to say "no" and not be pulled off course. On the other hand, the Controlling partner likes the Adapting partner's smooth sense of timing and appropriateness, knowing when to back off and come back later to win an argument or make a telling point.

Problems

With quick action on part of the Controlling partner and quick compromise by the Adapting partner, tough issues may get an insufficient hearing to be truly resolved. Resolution may be left to dangle until the Adapting partner just gets fed up with unstated resentment or concerns. The resentment can leak out in sarcastic jokes, put off promises and letting tasks go uncompleted.

Sensing this oblique resentment, the Controlling partner can become irritated or angry at the lack of directness and willingness to clear the air. In addition, glossing over important differences can lead to shallow commitment so that agreements fall apart. Important problems keep recurring, frustrating both partners.

Though the Adapting partner likes to be flexible and to experiment with new situations, there can be only modest changes, nothing too far out, to avoid the risk of failure. The Controlling partner's boldness, however, provides the driving force to take on big challenges.

While the Adapting partner may go along with a challenge, there is enough reluctance registered so that in the case of failure, the adapting partner can disavow responsibility for accepting the challenge. This can happen much to the surprise of the Controlling partner, leading to disappointment and disapproval of the Adapting partner.

The Work That Needs To Be Done

Important decisions need to be slowed down and the difficulties dug out. The Controlling partner needs to set a non-judgmental climate in which it is all right to disagree and in which persuasion and forcefulness are set aside until differences on the issues are aired.

The Adapting partner needs to be more direct and less concerned about possible disfavor for disagreeing. Often, indirect statements and humor diffuse the importance of what the Adapting partner is truly feeling. Indirect remarks and an engaging smile can then camouflage the Adapting partner's discomfort, as well as the meaning of the message.

Because their lives are so fast paced and filled with activity, both partners need to prioritize. This can help them define ahead of time what direction to take. They can also establish guidelines to tell if they are getting off course. This will give reassurance to the Adapting partner that he or she is on safe ground as long as priorities and predetermined guidelines are followed.

The Controlling partner's drive and energy needs to be focused and directed, limiting random challenges. Thrilling as new challenges may be for the Controlling partner, the Adapting one may be going along for the ride.

So, the Controlling partner needs to be more aware of the Adapting partner's unvoiced reactions. This will reduce some of the partner's burden of reluctantly slowing the pace by strongly disagreeing in order to be heard.

Conserving–Adapting

Attractions

The Conserving partner is admired for level-headed and logical approaches to living. Well thought out plans precede action and this offers the Adapting partner structure and direction to counterbalance his or her flexibility and desire to accommodate.

When the Adapting partner becomes emotional about issues or events, and starts flip flopping from one solution to another, the Conserving partner provides reason and factual information. This calms down the Adapting partner and provides focus. What is more, the Adapting partner appreciates the logical alternatives the Conserving partner naturally creates because it gives the Adapting partner a feeling of grounded flexibility.

What the Conserving partner admires is the Adapting partner's way of lightening up serious situations and stirring up some feelings around dull facts. The Adapting partner can make the ordinary sound extraordinary. If the Conserving partner's plans get convoluted and complicated, the Adapting partner can unravel and simplify them.

Awareness of what people are feeling is another area in which the Conserving partner appreciates the

Adapting pattern. Also, sensing the social dynamics in situations—who likes whom and what is causing tension—gives the Conserving partner a source of overlooked but useful information.

Problems

The complaints the Adapting partner experiences center on rigidity and too many rules, the lack of flexibility. Too much analyzing and not enough spontaneity is another complaint. Occasionally, the Adapting partner gets frustrated by the Conserving partner's seriousness and would appreciate more humor and a lighter touch.

At times, the Conserving partner seems unfriendly in social situations. This creates discomfort for the Adapting partner and he or she will try make up for that only to be surprised when the Conserving partner complains about trying too hard to be friendly and sociable.

When they are trying to plan or problem solve together, the Conserving partner complains that the Adapting partner breaks the train of thought with an ill-timed joke. The Adapting partner would rather be playful than serious and puts aside promises to follow strict agreements. According to the Conserving partner, this seems irresponsible and generates mistrust.

Finally, there is the conflict between too much and too little information. When the Adapting partner presents information upon which to make a decision, the Conserving partner can see it as sketchy and insufficient. When the reverse is true, the Adapting partner sees the information presented as over elaborate and confusing.

In a disagreement, the Conserving partner will state the information and the reasons, and then will retreat until the Adapting partner "sees the light," opens the issue again and agrees or comes up with better information or reasons. The Adapting partner can become somewhat weary pursuing and soliciting responses. To lighten the load, the Conserving partner needs to reach out earlier and accept a "less perfect" position in the service of the relationship.

The Work That Needs To Be Done

For the Conserving partner, he or she needs to entertain ideas with no immediate practical benefit. Also, select a low risk situation and "plunge" into it with minimal or no planning. While the apparent lack of control may be uncomfortable, the Adapting partner will be delighted that the Conserving partner let go and walked a moment in his or her shoes.

With regard to turning seriousness to friendliness, the Conserving partner needs to focus conversations on the other person and turn the desire for inquiry and information into a social tool. That is, spend less time giving information and more time gathering information on topics of interest to the other person.

The Adapting partner needs to take agreements more seriously and stick to them. It is important to acknowledge the other partner's exacting expectation about keeping one's word, and on occasions leave the casual attitude for matters which do not deeply concern the conserving partner.

Both partners need to find a middle ground on mutual tasks with a level of thoroughness and detail they can both tolerate. The Conserving partner should accept minimal information in order to save time; and the Adapting partner can give more complete information and do so without fear that flexibility will be narrowed by early disclosure of one's position.

Simple Complexity

Those are the pattern combinations, some alike, some different. Which combinations are best? The answer is in how we manage the unique issues generated by our similarities or differences.

Many of us have experienced relationships when we and our partner were the same and at other times when we were different. In the case of similarity, it was like looking into a mirror. We saw reflected back to us both what we liked and what we did not like in ourselves. When we were different from each other, it was as if the mirror was cracked and the image was fragmented, like a mixed up glass mosaic. We could not clearly make out the other person.

The quickest way to familiarize ourselves with another person is to understand their pattern. How that pattern impacts our own is the next step to better understanding.

Finally, doing the work that needs to be done with the combined patterns is the path to more satisfaction and less stress.

SUGGESTED READINGS

Aldwin, Carolyn M., Ph.D., *Stress, Coping, and Development,* The Guifford Press, New York, 1994.

Atkins, Stuart, Ph.D., *The Name of Your Game,* Business Consultants Network, New York, 2002.

Davis, Martha, Ph.D., Eshelman, Elizabeth Robbins, MSW, McKay, Matthew, Ph.D., *The Relaxation & Stress Reduction Workbook,* New Harbinger Publications, Inc., Oakland, CA., 2000.

Elkin, Allen, *Stress Management for Dummies,* IDG Books Worldwide, Inc., 1999.

Lazarus, Richard S., Ph.D., Tulkman, Susan, Ph.D., *Stress, Appraisal, and Coping,* Springer Publishing Company, New York, 1954.

Leyden-Rubinstein, Lori A., Ph.D., *The Stress Management Handbook,* Keats Publishing, Inc., 1998.

Luskin, Fred, Ph.D., Pelletter, Kenneth R., Ph.D., *Stress Free for Good,* Harpers Collins Publishers, New York, 2005.

Selye, Hans, MD., *The Stress of Life,* McGraw-Hill Book Company, New York, 1956.

Selye, Hans, MD., *Stress Without Distress,* New American Library, New York, 1975.

Sherman, Carl and the Editors of Prevention Magazine, *Stress Remedies,* St. Martin's Press, 1997.

Winner, Jay, MD., *Stress Management Made Simple,* Blue Mountain Press, Santa Barbara, CA., 2003

ABOUT THE AUTHOR

As a behavioral scientist, Dr. Stuart Atkins has consulted with and conducted self improvement workshops for many of the Fortune 500 companies, as well as churches, hospitals, government agencies and universities. His programs have benefited over 8 million people in over 20,000 organizations worldwide.

Before his graduate work, he was a marketing manager for Max Factor & Company, where he learned the practical realities of managing and organizational life.

Dr. Atkins has taught personal effectiveness, group dynamics, leadership and human factors in management at UCLA and the NTL Institute for Applied Behavioral Science.

Articles about his unique programs have appeared in such publications as Journal of Applied Behavioral Science, Chemical Engineering, Nation's Business, International Management Magazine and The Wall Street Journal.

Dr Atkins book **The Name of Your Game**, about personal effectiveness, managing stress, and relationships has been translated in other languages. In addition, he has written workbooks and materials for his programs, including **Solve It!** featuring problem solving to uproot stress at its source—troublesome problems and people.

His most recent self help program, **The Four Minute Feedback System®**, is a fully automated, interactive personal feedback system—online. It gathers information from family, friends, or coworkers about one's personal strengths and how to improve them.

People practice applying their feedback in various situations using unique online exercises.

At New York University, his undergraduate studies were in education and psychology. Post graduate studies were in industrial psychology at the University of Southern California where he was chosen to join the consulting firm of his graduate professors as Vice President of Psychological Services. Later, after establishing his own consulting company, he finished his doctoral work at the Union Institute and University in Applied Behavioral Science.

Other Works by Dr. Atkins:

A Moment in Forever
Bridge the Communication Gap
No Fault Accountability and the Blame Game
The Life Orientations® Method (LIFO®)
The Name of Your Game
T-Group for a Work Team
The Four Minute Feedback® System
Three Essentials for Effective Teamwork
Solve It! Solving Stressful Problems

WORKSHOP INFORMATION

SOLVE IT!—SOLVING STRESSFUL PROBLEMS

Workshops on Dr. Stuart Atkins' stress concepts of tolerating and solving stressful problems are available through the following worldwide training and consulting firm:

The Schutz Company
Marcia Johnson, VP of Customer Services
1-800-250-5357 (Direct)

THE LIFO® METHOD

Created by Dr. Stuart Atkins, the LIFO Method explores and capitalizes on people's personal strengths and styles, and orientations to life and work. It has spanned every kind of organization for over 40 years, and is utilized in 33 countries besides the U.S. It has helped people, at all organizational levels, to improve communications, personal productivity, teamwork and leadership.

THE HUMAN ELEMENT

The workshop focuses on self awareness, personal accountability, and building trust. Created 26 years ago by Dr. Will Schutz, it is an introduction to the many applications of the FIRO based instruments, which include developing personal and interpersonal effectiveness, improving customer service, resolving conflict, and teambuilding. Trainer Certification is also conducted worldwide.

RADICAL COLLABORATION

This takes adversarial confrontation out of negotiations and relationship disputes and replaces it with person to person or group to group collaborative relationship skills. It is a "radical" and powerful new approach to effective collaboration based on building trust and mutuality. It was created through the unique collaboration of psychologically oriented Judge James Tamm and Trainer-Therapist Ron Luyet.

ORDERING INFORMATION

For Additional Copies and Quantity Discounts:

Go to: www.stresslane.com
Call or write to the publisher:

Ashford Publishing

AP Ashford Publishing
8306 Wilshire Blvd. #990
Beverly Hills, CA 90211
323-650-5097
800-250-5357
www.stresslane.com
www.poweredbylifo.com